JESSE JACKSON

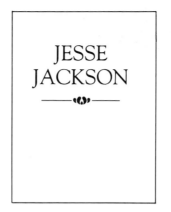

JESSE JACKSON

◖◗

Robert Jakoubek

Senior Consulting Editor
Nathan Irvin Huggins
Director
*W.E.B. Du Bois Institute for Afro-American Research
Harvard University*

CHELSEA HOUSE PUBLISHERS
New York   Philadelphia

Chelsea House Publishers
Editor-in-Chief Remmel Nunn
Managing Editor Karyn Gullen Browne
Copy Chief Juliann Barbato
Picture Editor Adrian G. Allen
Art Director Maria Epes
Deputy Copy Chief Mark Rifkin
Assistant Art Director Noreen Romano
Manufacturing Manager Gerald Levine
Systems Manager Lindsey Ottman
Production Manager Joseph Romano
Production Coordinator Marie Claire Cebrián

Black Americans of Achievement
Senior Editor Richard Rennert

Staff for JESSE JACKSON
Text Editor Marian W. Taylor
Copy Editor Brian Sookram
Editorial Assistant Michele Haddad
Picture Researcher Joan Beard
Designer Ghila Krajzman
Cover Illustration Daniel Mark Duffy

5 7 9 8 6

Library of Congress Cataloging-in-Publication Data
Jakoubek, Robert E.
     Jesse Jackson: civil rights leader and politician/by Robert Jakoubek.
       p.   cm.—(Black Americans of achievement)
     Includes bibliographical references and index.
     Summary: Examines the life and political career of Jesse Jackson.
     ISBN 0-7910-1130-5
          0-7910-1155-0 (pbk.)
     1. Jackson, Jesse, 1941– —Juvenile literature. 2. Afro-
Americans—Biography—Juvenile literature. 3. Civil rights
workers—United States—Biography——Juvenile literature. 4.
Presidential candidates—United States—Biography—Juvenile
literature. [1. Jackson, Jesse, 1941- . 2. Civil right
workers. 3. Afro-Americans—Biography.] I. Title. II. Series.
E185.97.J25J35 1991   91-7378
973.927'092—dc92 —dc20   CIP
[B]   AC

*Frontispiece: Admirers reach out
to Jesse Jackson in Philadelphia.
By the early 1990s, he had firmly
established himself as the nation's
leading black spokesperson.*

CONTENTS

BLACK AMERICANS OF ACHIEVEMENT

Ralph Abernathy
civil rights leader

Muhammad Ali
heavyweight champion

Richard Allen
religious leader and social activist

Louis Armstrong
musician

Arthur Ashe
tennis great

Josephine Baker
entertainer

James Baldwin
author

Benjamin Banneker
scientist and mathematician

Amiri Baraka
poet and playwright

Count Basie
bandleader and composer

Romare Bearden
artist

James Beckwourth
frontiersman

Mary McLeod Bethune
educator

Blanche Bruce
politician

Ralph Bunche
diplomat

George Washington Carver
botanist

Charles Chesnutt
author

Bill Cosby
entertainer

Paul Cuffe
merchant and abolitionist

Father Divine
religious leader

Frederick Douglass
abolitionist editor

Charles Drew
physician

W.E.B. Du Bois
scholar and activist

Paul Laurence Dunbar
poet

Katherine Dunham
dancer and choreographer

Marian Wright Edelman
civil rights leader and lawyer

Duke Ellington
bandleader and composer

Ralph Ellison
author

Julius Erving
basketball great

James Farmer
civil rights leader

Ella Fitzgerald
singer

Marcus Garvey
black-nationalist leader

Dizzy Gillespie
musician

Prince Hall
social reformer

W. C. Handy
father of the blues

William Hastie
educator and politician

Matthew Henson
explorer

Chester Himes
author

Billie Holiday
singer

John Hope
educator

Lena Horne
entertainer

Langston Hughes
poet

Zora Neale Hurston
author

Jesse Jackson
civil rights leader and politician

Jack Johnson
heavyweight champion

James Weldon Johnson
author

Scott Joplin
composer

Barbara Jordan
politician

Martin Luther King, Jr.
civil rights leader

Alain Locke
scholar and educator

Joe Louis
heavyweight champion

Ronald McNair
astronaut

Malcolm X
militant black leader

Thurgood Marshall
Supreme Court justice

Elijah Muhammad
religious leader

Jesse Owens
champion athlete

Charlie Parker
musician

Gordon Parks
photographer

Sidney Poitier
actor

Adam Clayton Powell, Jr.
political leader

Leontyne Price
opera singer

A. Philip Randolph
labor leader

Paul Robeson
singer and actor

Jackie Robinson
baseball great

Bill Russell
basketball great

John Russwurm
publisher

Sojourner Truth
antislavery activist

Harriet Tubman
antislavery activist

Nat Turner
slave revolt leader

Denmark Vesey
slave revolt leader

Madam C. J. Walker
entrepreneur

Booker T. Washington
educator

Harold Washington
politician

Walter White
civil rights leader and author

Richard Wright
author

ON
ACHIEVEMENT

———— ⬧ ————

Coretta Scott King

BEFORE YOU BEGIN this book, I hope you will ask yourself what the word excellence means to you. I think that it's a question we should all ask, and keep asking as we grow older and change. Because the truest answer to it should never change. When you think of excellence, perhaps you think of success at work; or of becoming wealthy; or meeting the right person, getting married, and having a good family life.

Those important goals are worth striving for, but there is a better way to look at excellence. As Martin Luther King, Jr., said in one of his last sermons, "I want you to be first in love. I want you to be first in moral excellence. I want you to be first in generosity. If you want to be important, wonderful. If you want to be great, wonderful. But recognize that he who is greatest among you shall be your servant."

My husband, Martin Luther King, Jr., knew that the true meaning of achievement is service. When I met him, in 1952, he was already ordained as a Baptist preacher and was working towards a doctoral degree at Boston University. I was studying at the New England Conservatory and dreamed of accomplishments in music. We married a year later, and after I graduated the following year we moved to Montgomery, Alabama. We didn't know it then, but our notions of achievement were about to undergo a dramatic change.

You may have read or heard about what happened next. What began with the boycott of a local bus line grew into a national movement, and by the time he was assassinated in 1968 my husband had fashioned a black movement powerful enough to shatter forever the practice of racial segregation. What you may not have read about is where he got his method for resisting injustice without compromising his religious beliefs.

7

He adopted the strategy of nonviolence from a man of a different race, who lived in a distant country, and even practiced a different religion. The man was Mahatma Gandhi, the great leader of India, who devoted his life to serving humanity in the spirit of love and nonviolence. It was in these principles that Martin discovered his method for social reform. More than anything else, those two principles were the key to his achievements.

This book is about black Americans who served society through the excellence of their achievements. It forms a part of the rich history of black men and women in America—a history of stunning accomplishments in every field of human endeavor, from literature and art to science, industry, education, diplomacy, athletics, jurisprudence, even polar exploration.

Not all of the people in this history had the same ideals, but I think you will find something that all of them have in common. Like Martin Luther King, Jr., they all decided to become "drum majors" and serve humanity. In that principle—whether it was expressed in books, inventions, or song—they found something outside themselves to use as a goal and a guide. Something that showed them a way to serve others, instead of living only for themselves.

Reading the stories of these courageous men and women not only helps us discover the principles that we will use to guide our own lives but also teaches us about our black heritage and about America itself. It is crucial for us to know the heroes and heroines of our history and to realize that the price we paid in our struggle for equality in America was dear. But we must also understand that we have gotten as far as we have partly because America's democratic system and ideals made it possible.

We are still struggling with racism and prejudice. But the great men and women in this series are a tribute to the spirit of our democratic ideals and the system in which they have flourished. And that makes their stories special and worth knowing.

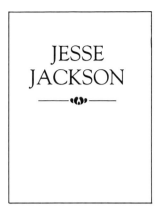

JESSE
JACKSON

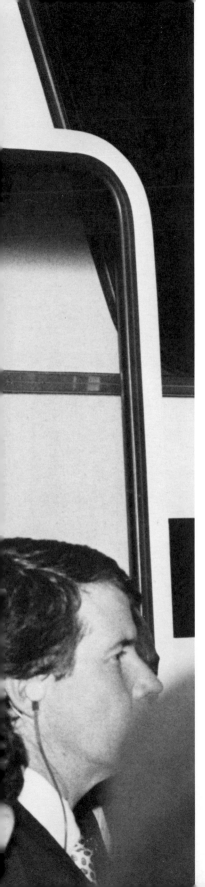

1

RAINBOW EXPRESS

SHORTLY AFTER LUNCHTIME on July 14, 1988, a blazing summer afternoon, the Reverend Jesse L. Jackson departed Chicago for the Democratic National Convention in Atlanta. He was, so far as anyone could recall, the first person seeking the presidential nomination of a major American political party to go to its national convention by bus.

It was, to be sure, not Greyhound he traveled. His vehicle was a nicely appointed motor coach with a kitchen, television sets, and two spacious seating areas. On the outside, beneath the bus windows, several Jackson for President signs held the smiling likeness of the candidate and advertised the point of the trip. Jackson would be leading a parade of 7 chartered buses—the Rainbow Express—on the 715-mile journey southward.

Climbing aboard, Jackson hoisted a thumbs-up gesture to the small band of admirers on the sidewalk, waved to the considerably larger group of reporters and photographers, then gave his wife a farewell kiss.

Presidential hopeful Jesse Jackson, traveling by Rainbow Express—a seven-bus cavalcade—to the 1988 Democratic National Convention in Atlanta, stops to greet well-wishers in Houston, Texas. Accompanying the Chicagoan on his 715-mile trip to Atlanta were relatives, aides, friends, and 125 journalists.

11

Jacqueline Jackson, as her husband later noted, possessed the "good sense" to travel to Atlanta by plane.

Inside the bus, Jackson threaded his way through his children, his aides, and his friends toward one of the deeply cushioned seats. Dressed in jeans and a white polo shirt, he looked perhaps 15 years younger than his age of 46 and he moved with the ease of a college quarterback.

His face, with its wide-set eyes and trimmed mustache, and his voice, with its rhythmic cadences learned in the black churches of the Deep South, were among the best known in America. For two decades, Jackson had been a presence on the national scene, first as a lieutenant of Martin Luther King, Jr., during the civil rights movement of the 1960s, then as the founder of a social reform organization called People United to Serve Humanity (PUSH). And always, and seemingly everywhere, Jackson appeared as the outspoken foe of what he perceived to be racism, imperialism, and economic injustice.

In 1984, responding to the plea, "Run, Jesse, Run," Jackson had sought the Democratic presidential nomination, representing what he called a Rainbow Coalition of blacks, of the poor, of women, of homosexuals, of the unemployed. His campaign captured the fevered attention of the media and whipped up powerful storms of controversy; still, he had finished far behind Walter Mondale in the Democratic presidential sweepstakes.

Jackson kept right on running, and in 1988, to no one's surprise, he again became a candidate for president. But this time, to everyone's surprise, he won primaries and swept caucuses. At the Democratic convention in Atlanta, he would have 1,200 delegates committed to his name.

He had outrun and outlasted every Democratic hopeful except one: Governor Michael S. Dukakis of Massachusetts. Then, in a series of spring primaries from New York to California, Dukakis and Jackson had gone head to head, and the diminutive governor had soundly whipped the tall preacher. As Jackson left Chicago for Atlanta, it was all over but the shouting. Controlling the votes of 2,800 delegates, Dukakis had the nomination locked up.

Jackson had nevertheless pressed ahead with his campaign, refusing to concede, passing up every chance to get behind Dukakis. By staying in the race, Jackson hoped to pressure Dukakis into selecting him as his running mate. Jackson believed that by making such a strong showing for the presidency, he had staked a claim to the vice-presidential nomination. He stated his case: If the vice-presidential nominee should be "someone who can mobilize a mass of Democrats, I've done that. If it's someone who is not limited to regional appeal, I've won primaries from Vermont to Puerto Rico, from Mississippi to Michigan, from Texas to Alaska."

But Michael Dukakis had not the slightest intention of picking Jesse Jackson. In the first place, every public opinion poll showed that a Dukakis-Jackson ticket would be doomed; too many white voters would desert it for the Republicans. Furthermore, Dukakis did not want as his vice-president a man who had never held public office, who stood considerably to Dukakis's left on most matters of policy, and whose charisma and eloquence vastly exceeded his own.

Yet Dukakis had to give the *impression* he was seriously considering Jackson. To have done otherwise would have been a slap in the face to Jackson and Jackson's loyal supporters. And if they, the black Democrats who had nearly unanimously backed Jackson in the primaries, did not vote for Dukakis in November, the governor was sure to lose.

On the Fourth of July, Dukakis had attempted to cultivate his rival. The governor and his wife, Kitty, invited Jesse and Jacqueline Jackson to their home

Jackson and his wife, Jackie, attend a Boston Pops concert with Massachusetts governor Michael Dukakis on the Fourth of July, 1988. All smiles on the surface, the Jacksons were inwardly raging about what they considered high-handed treatment from Dukakis, at this point the almost certain Democratic presidential candidate.

just outside Boston for a holiday dinner, followed by the annual Boston Pops concert and fireworks display on the Charles River.

Nothing went right. The Jacksons arrived an hour and a half late, partly because no one met them at Logan Airport. The Dukakises, unaware of Jackson's allergy to milk, served a meal of creamy New England clam chowder and salmon poached in milk. And just when Dukakis and his guest settled down in the living room to discuss the vice-presidency, the governor's daughters entered the room, offering ice cream for dessert. At the concert, a famished Jackson ordered fried chicken from a vendor and Dukakis strained to make small talk. There was, of course, a chance for some serious political talk after the concert, but Dukakis said he felt sleepy.

The evening left Jackson in a foul mood. "He felt he had been treated like a nigger," said a friend.

Compared to what happened next, the dinner was a stunning social success. The governor and his campaign continued the charade that Jackson was under serious consideration for vice-president. Dukakis dispatched his senior adviser, Paul Brountas, to conduct a lengthy interview with Jackson. At its conclusion, Brountas said that whomever Dukakis selected, Jackson would be among the first to know, well before the choice became public. "Reverend Jackson," Brountas pledged, "you're not going to read about it in the newspapers."

To be fair, he did not. He heard the news from a reporter. On the morning of Wednesday, July 13, as he disembarked from a plane at National Airport in Washington, D.C., newspeople closed in, each asking what he thought of Dukakis's choosing Senator Lloyd Bentsen of Texas to be his running mate.

Jackson was dumbstruck. His jaw tightly set, obviously trying to control his temper, he pushed past the reporters and said nothing. Later in the day, he explained that he was really not upset about having been left in the dark. "No, I'm too controlled," he said. "I'm too clear. I'm too mature to be angry. I am focused on what we must do to keep hope alive." For once, his words were entirely unpersuasive. He appeared very angry.

From Dukakis's headquarters in Boston came the lame explanation that it had all been a foul-up. No offense had been intended; staff members just could not locate in time the telephone number of the Cincinnati hotel where Jackson had spent the night. Jackson supporters were not buying it. Many believed it to be a calculated snub. "They weren't simply careless," said Maxine Waters of California.

There matters stood when the Rainbow Express rolled out of Chicago on its way to Atlanta. Jackson,

Meeting reporters in Washington, D.C., on July 13, 1988, Jackson learns that Michael Dukakis has bypassed him in selecting a running mate; only days earlier, the probable Democratic presidential nominee had promised to inform Jackson privately about his choice for vice-president. Although Jackson claimed he was "too mature to be angry" about the selection of Texas senator Lloyd Bentsen, he was visibly steamed by Dukakis's method of handling it.

leader of the Democratic party's left wing, obviously felt shunned, not only by Dukakis's apparent discourtesy but by the selection of Bentsen, a conservative Texan. "Mr. Bentsen represents one wing of the party, I represent the other wing," Jackson proclaimed. "It takes two wings to fly, and so far, our wing is not connected."

The Democratic convention appeared headed for a crash landing. Party leaders desperately wanted a harmonious, united show in Atlanta, and Jackson was promising to give them anything but. In the Jackson camp, there was talk of demonstrations in the streets of Atlanta, of divisive fights over the party platform, even of Jackson himself challenging Bentsen for the vice-presidential nomination from the floor of the convention. "This party was hanging by a thread in Atlanta," Jackson's aide Ron Brown recalled.

As the Rainbow Express roared southward along Interstate 65, the mood in the candidate's motor coach was surprisingly upbeat. Jackson's five children lifted everyone's spirits. "It's fun. It's family time. We laugh a lot," said one daughter.

More than 125 reporters, photographers, and television crew members squeezed onto the buses, and their presence guaranteed Jackson a prominent place on the evening news and in the next morning's newspapers. The bus caravan was meant as a plain reminder of the Freedom Rides of the early 1960s, the time when young blacks, traveling on interstate buses into the Deep South, challenged the racial segregation found in the facilities of public transportation.

Late on Thursday afternoon, July 14, the Rainbow Express rumbled into Indianapolis. Only a few curious pedestrians turned to watch the buses pass by, but that evening at a rally in the Christ Missionary Baptist Church, Jackson found the sort of enthusiasm and acclaim that had long sustained his campaigns. He was, after all, a preacher, and these were his people—the devout black churchgoers who had been the first to raise the cry: "Run, Jesse, Run."

Handmade Jackson for President signs decorated the walls and hung from the church balcony. More than 1,000 people filled the church, which had no air-conditioning, on one of the hottest nights of the hottest summer in a half century. "I was born against the odds," Jackson cried, sweat pouring from his face. "I grew up against the odds. I stand here against the odds. I am an odds breaker and a dream maker. I will never surrender."

The next morning, the Rainbow Express moved southward once more, sweeping past the brown fields of corn and soybeans stunted by the summer's drought. At all times, several black Mercury sedans— the vehicles of the Secret Service agents assigned to protect Jackson—kept pace alongside the candidate's bus. In Louisville and Nashville on Friday and in Chattanooga on Saturday, Jackson stopped for rallies at the way stations of his campaign, the black churches. At each, in words nearly identical to those he had spoken in Indianapolis, he defiantly expressed his aims.

Frequently, the helicopters of local television stations hovered above the Rainbow Express, collecting shots of the caravan for evening news broadcasts. The missed phone call, and Jackson's response to it, kept the spotlight trained on him, and he was doing nothing to lessen the tension between himself and Dukakis. At one point, he suggested that former president Jimmy Carter might mediate his dispute with the governor. Dukakis flatly rejected the idea.

Early Saturday afternoon, July 16, the express pulled up alongside Interstate 75 in Calhoun, Georgia, for two passengers. One was Bert Lance, a beefy, freewheeling Georgian who had briefly directed the federal budget during the Carter administration. Over the last few years, he had emerged as an unlikely but influential Jackson adviser. The other new passenger was Dan Rather, the high-strung, high-powered anchorman of CBS News.

At the side of the highway, oblivious to the horrendous traffic jam the stopped buses were causing, Jackson and Rather embraced and exchanged pleasantries. What could say more about Jackson's place at the center of things? Dan Rather, the most famous newsperson in America, had come to him and was riding his bus to the Democratic convention.

Arriving in Atlanta four hours late, the Rainbow Express proceeded to Piedmont Park, where several thousand Jackson partisans had been patiently waiting all afternoon. Nearly a century before, on the same spot, Booker T. Washington had delivered his famous "Atlanta Compromise" speech, in which he urged his fellow blacks to exchange political and social equality for economic advancement.

Compromise was not on Jesse Jackson's mind. He demanded a significant place for himself and his supporters in the Democratic party. He requested equity, partnership, and shared responsibility. "I don't mind working," he said of his role in the party. "I'll go out and pick the voters. I'll go back and bale up some votes. But when I get to the Big House, I want to help count the cotton."

He had stretched his pique with Dukakis too far. His remarks in Piedmont Park clearly cast him as the field hand and Dukakis, the man in the "Big House," as the slaveholder. And what did he mean when he proposed partnership and shared responsibility? After all, there were two, not three, places on the national ticket.

If Jackson had any desire for a large future in the Democratic party—and he most certainly did—the time had come to fold his hand. If he continued to shun Dukakis, he would be remembered as the man who wrecked the Democratic convention and spoiled the party's chances for victory in November. In a profession that places an extravagant value on party loyalty, such a memory would be hard to overcome.

Hardly a political innocent, Jackson knew this as well as anyone. So, on Sunday evening, July 17, when a telephone call from Dukakis reached him at the Fox Theatre, where he was attending a gospel concert, he readily took it in a backstage holding room. And when the governor proposed a breakfast meeting the next morning at 8:30, he quickly agreed to be there.

On Monday morning, in Dukakis's suite at the Hyatt Regency, over a breakfast of cereal, fruit, and coffee, the two rivals got down to brass tacks. The atmosphere was decidedly uncomfortable. Dukakis griped about Jackson's "Big House" remark, saying he did not appreciate being compared to a slaveholder. Jackson, in no uncertain words, deplored the missed phone call. For several hours, it went back and forth. "They got it out on the table and they cleared the air," said a Jackson associate.

In the late morning, Lloyd Bentsen joined the meeting; soon afterward, the three men, wreathed in smiles, appeared together at a press conference in the hotel basement. Dukakis complimented Jackson. Jackson complimented Dukakis. And then, in a moment everyone had been waiting for, Jackson pledged his support for the Dukakis-Bentsen ticket and promised a harmonious convention. There would be no demonstrations, a minimum of dissent over the party platform, and no opposition to Bentsen's nomination for vice-president.

And what had Jackson received in return for his cooperation? Precious little. Dukakis did not budge an inch when it came to issues of foreign and domestic policy, making no attempt to accommodate Jackson's agenda. Nor did he offer Jackson a job in a Dukakis administration. All Jackson got were some

Delegate Julia Hicks leads a cheer for her candidate on the last day of the 1988 convention. Even at this point, no one was sure what to expect from Jackson: Would he continue to shun Dukakis, or would he urge his backers to support the ticket? Not until his rousing speech at the end of the convention did Jackson make his intentions clear.

changes in party rules concerning the selection of convention delegates for 1992, an assurance that members of his staff would be employed by the Dukakis campaign, and, for himself, the use of a chartered plane during the fall campaign.

Seeing Dukakis and Jackson arm in arm at the press conference, most Democrats breathed a sigh of relief. Their party was whole again. Among Jackson's ardent partisans, however, the feelings were rather different. "A plane for Jesse to campaign for Dukakis. So what?" snorted a Jackson delegate from Mississippi. Hosea Williams, an old ally from the civil rights movement, saw matters in a similar light: "Basically, Dukakis got Jesse in that meeting and told Jesse to go to hell."

For the media, Jackson put up a brave front, denying that he had lost a thing, but his family and his closest advisers knew he was depressed. His campaign was over. He had, for all the world to see, come out second best in his altercation with Dukakis. All that remained for him in Atlanta was his speech to the convention on Tuesday night.

Prior to the speech, Jackson recalled, several party officials asked him which governor or senator he would like to have present him to the convention. "None of them," he replied. "Who do you want then?" they asked. "The Jackson Five," he said. A singing group? "The Jackson Five I'm referring to are my kids."

On Tuesday evening, before a throng bursting the seams of Atlanta's Omni Center, the five Jackson children, Jacqueline, Yusef, Jonathan, Santita, and Jesse, Jr., one after the other, came to the rostrum and spoke of their father. "We, the children of Jesse and Jacqueline Jackson, are proud to be Jacksons," proclaimed Jesse, Jr.

At three minutes before 11 o'clock eastern time, Jesse Jackson, dressed in a dark gray pin-striped suit; a pale blue shirt with a highly starched, long-pointed

His image projected on the huge television screens above him, Jackson (center) rocks listeners with his powerful convention address. In the 55-minute speech, repeatedly interrupted with cheers and applause, Jackson reached out to the nation's poor and pledged to support the Democratic ticket.

collar; and a red tie with white polka dots, stepped to the microphones. He smiled and showed the thumbs-up sign to the delegates and spectators in the hall. They cheered him madly and waved red-and-white Jesse! signs.

At last, when the demonstration showed signs of subsiding, Jackson started to speak. His voice was hoarse. "When I look out at this convention, I see the face of America, red, yellow, brown, black, and white. We are all precious in God's sight—the real rainbow coalition."

From his front-row box seat, Jimmy Carter listened intently. Fifty-five minutes later, when Jackson finished, the former president would say he had just heard "the best speech ever given at a convention, certainly in my lifetime."

Jackson spoke of his mentor, now 20 years dead: "Dr. Martin Luther King, Jr., lies only a few miles from us tonight. Tonight he must feel good as he looks down upon us. We sit here together, a rainbow, a coalition—the sons and daughters of slave masters and the sons and daughters of slaves sitting together around a common table, to decide the direction of our party and our country. His heart would be full tonight."

In her seat, Coretta Scott King, the great man's widow and someone who had always been wary of Jackson, brushed away a tear.

The hoarseness had vanished from Jackson's voice. So had the petulance that had colored his dispute with Michael Dukakis. He spoke of love and common ground, of unity and working together. To the enormous television audience, mostly white and mostly middle class, he described his people—the poor and the dispossessed.

"Most poor people are not on welfare. . . . I know. I live amongst them. I'm one of them. I know they work. I'm a witness. They catch the early bus. They work every day. They raise other people's children. They work every day. They clean the streets. They work every day. They drive vans with cabs. They work every day. They change the beds you slept in in these hotels last night and can't get a union contract. They work every day."

His voice now exploding into a shout, now retreating to a husky whisper, Jackson had the audience in the palm of his hand.

In a modest two-bedroom apartment in southeast Atlanta, Betty Strozier sat close to her television set, not wanting to miss a word of Jackson's speech. Now and then she clasped her hands and silently nodded. For the past 19 years, she had raised 3 sons by herself. She worked every day as a seamstress, and she made

$9,000 a year. "We don't have a lot, but what we have is ours," she said. "Black people have always learned to make do."

An Atlanta cabdriver said that during the speech "not a driver drove, not a hooker hooked. We all found bars with TVs."

Proudly, Jackson spoke of himself: "I know abandonment and people being mean to you, and saying you're nothing and nobody, and can never be anything. I understand. . . . I'm adopted. When I had no name, my grandmother gave me her name. . . . So I wouldn't have a blank space, she gave me a name to hold me over. I understand when you have no name. . . .

"Born in a three-room house, bathroom in the backyard, slop jar by the bed, no hot and cold running water. I understand. . . .

"My mother, a working woman. So many days she went to work early with runs in her stockings. She knew better, but she wore runs in her stockings so that my brother and I could have matching socks and not be laughed at at school. . . .

"Every one of these funny labels they put on you, those of you who are watching this broadcast tonight in the projects, on the corners, I understand. Call you outcast, low down, you can't make it, you're nothing, you're from nobody, subclass, underclass—when you see Jesse Jackson, when my name goes in nomination, your name goes in nomination."

For at least the 50th time, the Democratic convention applauded his words. He was nearly finished. "You must not surrender," he said. "You may or may not get there, but just know that you're qualified and you hold on and hold out. We must never surrender. America will get better and better. Keep hope alive. Keep hope alive. Keep hope alive. On tomorrow night and beyond, keep hope alive.

"I love you very much. I love you very much." ❧

2

THE DRIVING FORCE

TALL AND GRACEFUL, with a fine figure, Helen Burns was one of the prettiest girls in Greenville, South Carolina. What's more, she had the best singing voice in her class at Sterling High School, a voice so good that eventually five music colleges offered her scholarships. But during the spring of 1941, when she was 16, her hopes for a singing career and her dreams of a brighter life turned to dust. She found out she was pregnant, and because of that, she faced dishonor and shame.

She faced it first at home. Her mother, Matilda Burns, had been through the same thing herself, having as a teenager borne Helen out of wedlock. Ever since, she prayed Helen would avoid her own fate—no husband, hard days working as a maid for a white family, never having enough time or money or anything else. Enraged at her daughter, she offered nothing in the way of sympathy. "It's your responsibility," she said.

Matters were just as bad at church. Word of Helen's pregnancy spread quickly, and when it got to the worshipers at the Springfield Baptist Church, they voted to expel her from the congregation. Only later, when she confessed, "I have sinned against the church," was she restored to membership. And as if

Jesse Burns, pictured here at the age of 13, became Jesse Jackson when his mother's husband, Charles Jackson, legally adopted him in 1957. Fond of Jackson, the boy also developed a warm relationship with his blood father, Noah Robinson, Sr.

25

her mother's anger and the church's hard heart were not sufficient, Helen had to endure the sneers of her classmates and the scorn of family and townspeople. Thirty years later, a relative would still speak of Helen's pregnancy as "this terrible, dishonorable disgrace."

Who could blame her for running away? With the baby's father, she fled to Chicago. But escape proved to be no solution, and before long she returned to Greenville, hearing once more her mother say the coming baby was "your responsibility."

"I gladly accepted," Helen recalled years later. "I said, O.K., that singing career is over. I was committed to being a real mother."

Early on the morning of October 8, 1941, Matilda Burns sent for a midwife, Minnie Mason, and at 9:00 A.M., she delivered Helen's baby, a 7-pound, 4-ounce boy. "It seemed the child was in a hurry to get here," Mason said. "By the time the doctor arrived, I had just wrapped him in a blanket and laid him in bed with his mother." Helen and Matilda named the infant Jesse Louis Burns, his first two names coming from his father's side of the family.

"He was a charmer from the start," said a neighbor. "Always causing everything. He'd give you a little old sexy smile. I couldn't stand it. I'd run up those steps and bite him."

Two years after her son's birth, on October 2, 1943, Helen married Charles Jackson, a 24-year-old postal worker. Like millions of other wartime newlyweds, the Jacksons had only a brief time together. Charles, who had been drafted into the armed services, was dispatched to his unit shortly after the wedding. As everyone in the black neighborhoods of Greenville seemed to know, Charles was not Jesse's father. Yet Helen wanted her son to believe otherwise. Time and again, she showed little Jesse a photograph of Charles in his soldier's uniform and said, "Your father's coming home soon."

When Jackson did come home from the war, he followed his wife's lead. "I never told him I was not his father because I didn't want him to grow up thinking he was different," Jackson recalled. "At four and five years old he was calling me Daddy, following me around, tugging at my knee."

The neighborhood children were less accommodating. By the time Jesse was about six, they had begun a cruel taunting on the playground at Happy Hearts Park. "Your daddy ain't none of your daddy," they chanted at Jesse. "You ain't nothing but a no-body, nothing but a no-body."

In tears, Jesse would run home to his mother's embrace. "He cried a lot," she remembered. "He would try to be very brave. He never came home and repeated the things they said—you had to read the expression on his face." Bit by bit, from his mother, from his grandmother, from his playmates, Jesse found out the truth, and he stopped calling Charles Jackson "Daddy."

Jesse did not have to look far to find his blood father. Noah Robinson was one of the best-known black men in Greenville, and at the time of Jesse's birth, he lived right next door to Matilda Burns and her daughter, Helen. "I didn't have any children by my own wife," Robinson said years later. "Helen, she was pretty, she was a baby—we just got to liking each other, and it all started. Then Helen said to me, 'I'll have a child for you.' I said, 'Well, you know I'm married, I can't do that kind of thing.' Well, it happened. Everybody in town knew."

And everyone talked about it. But Robinson was not one to let the gossip of a small town get in his way. He was a man on the move and he was after success. When Jesse came to know him as his blood father, Robinson was a valued employee of the Ryan

Greenville, South Carolina (pictured on a postcard from the early 1940s), was a pleasant, quiet city of 60,000 residents when Jackson was born there in 1941. Like other southern communities of the era, however, Greenville was also a city of strictly enforced racial segregation.

textile mill and had settled his family into Greenville's best black neighborhood. His fieldstone house, the one with a wrought-iron *R* on the chimney, sat on a large, shady corner lot and had a basketball court in back and a brick wall in front and along the sides.

Tall, barrel chested, and brown skinned, Robinson had as a young man fought his way to a Golden Gloves championship. Long after hanging up the boxing gloves, he stayed a slugger, becoming particularly combative if he was on the receiving end of a racial slur. As one of his sons would say years later, "Few whites got funny with Daddy. He'd punch them out." Once, at the Ryan mill, a white executive gave a few pokes to Robinson's posterior. In a flash, Robinson spun around and launched a right hook that knocked his tormentor out cold.

For punching a white, let alone a white boss, virtually every other southern black would have been fired instantly, perhaps even driven out of town. Not Noah Robinson. He had the good fortune to be employed by John J. Ryan. Remarkably, the mill owner fired the white executive, explaining that he liked Robinson's spirit. During the years that followed, Ryan continued to patronize and promote Robinson. When Robinson wished to take his family to Philadelphia for a summer visit, it was Ryan who bought them first-class tickets on the Crescent, the premier train of the Southern Railway.

Thereafter, the Robinsons took the Crescent to Philadelphia every summer, no one among them enjoying the trip more than Noah Robinson, Jr., who was 10 months younger than Jesse Burns. Noah, Jr., seemed to have been born lucky. He inherited his father's golden brown skin and aquiline nose, lived in the fine house with its own basketball court, and when it came to his education, had John J. Ryan pulling strings to gain his entry into an exclusive Catholic school.

When he was seven or eight, young Noah became aware of his half brother, Jesse. "I was playing on the playground with a group of boys and some lady called me over," he recalled. "She whispered to me, 'See that kid over there with the curly hair, well, he's your brother.' " At home that evening, said Noah, Jr., his father "sank down in the telephone chair and explained what had happened."

All along, Robinson had kept track of Jesse, often going to the playground or schoolyard to watch him from a distance. Now and then, he slipped Helen Jackson some money for the boy, and each Thanksgiving and Christmas he sent her an overflowing basket of seasonal delicacies. But Noah's wife drew the line at any closer relationship. Unsurprisingly, she had no desire to be reminded of her husband's affair with Helen. "I'd want to be with him so bad," Robinson said of Jesse.

Jesse felt the same way. There were days when he would sneak up to the fieldstone house with the wrought-iron *R* on the chimney and stare into a window, hoping to catch a glimpse of his father. "Sometimes I wouldn't see him right away and Noah

Junior would tell me he was out there," Robinson recalled. "No telling how long he could have been there. As soon as I would go to the window and wave, he would wave back and run away."

Jesse was never invited in, and when the Robinsons left for their annual summer vacation in Philadelphia, Jesse stayed in Greenville, feeling miserable and deserted. "I didn't know until Jesse was a big boy that he used to cry when the rest of us would take off and leave him behind," Robinson said.

Eventually, the Robinsons and Jacksons patched things up. By the time Jesse was a teenager, he was a regular and welcome visitor to his blood father's home. But those early years of rejection, of being told by his playmates he was a "nobody," of always being on the outside looking in, left their mark.

"If your father says my blood is your blood, but really you're denied, it has to affect you on the inside," Jesse's schoolboy coach said nearly 40 years later. "If you've got a lot of pride, and Jesse has that, this can get painful. I think that was the driving force behind whatever he's done."

Having seen the well-to-do Robinsons, Jesse knew he was missing a great deal. "You sense these distinctions," he told writer Gail Sheehy in 1987. "You long for the privileges other people have." In truth, the Jacksons had more than most. Charles earned a steady $3,000 per year from the post office, and Helen, who had attended beauty college after giving up on a singing career, brought in additional income as a hairdresser.

"We were never poor," Charles Jackson insisted. "We never wanted for anything. We've never been on welfare, because I was never without a job. We never begged anybody for a dime. And my family never went hungry a day in their lives."

Jackson provided his stepson with more than financial support: In 1957, when Jesse was 16, he legally adopted him. By then, Jesse had come to love the man he called Charlie Henry. He later dedicated a collection of his speeches "to Charles Jackson, who adopted me and gave me his name, his love, his encouragement, discipline and a high sense of self-respect."

Until Jesse was in the sixth grade, the Jacksons lived on University Ridge Street, near Furman University, in a three-room cottage with a coal bin beneath the floorboards and a toilet on the back porch. In the early 1950s, they moved to Fieldcrest Village, which the city directory of the time described as "a housing project for the colored located at the end of Greenacre Road." The federally funded complex consisted of square brick buildings divided into two-story row houses. It was a step up in the world for the Jacksons. Their home had a living room and kitchen downstairs and two bedrooms and a bath upstairs. They needed the larger space; it was also home for Helen's mother, Matilda, and for Jesse's half brothers, Charles and George.

The black neighborhoods of Greenville were tightly knit and self-supporting. "There were two or three people in the neighborhood who just kept big

Sterling High School's popular football coach, Joseph D. Mathis, counsels Jackson (center) and his teammates during halftime of a 1957 game. Mathis spotted Jackson as a winner early on: "I told him he was going to be heir apparent to great things," recalled the coach of his star quarterback.

pots of vegetable soup on," Jesse Jackson recalled. "When folks didn't have any food, they couldn't go to the Salvation Army because they were black. They couldn't get Social Security; they couldn't get welfare. But folks had a tradition of being kind to one another, because that was our roots."

Matilda Burns, matriarch of the house and called Aunt Tibby by nearly everyone, took a particular interest in Jesse. She told him he was special, that someday he would be some*body*: "Nothing is impossible for those who love the Lord," she said. "Come hell or high water, if you got the guts, boy, ain't nothing or nobody can turn you around." Above all, she taught him never to forsake hope. "So, every goodbye ain't gone," she would say. "Just hold on; there's joy coming in the morning."

Early on, Jesse showed signs of realizing his grandmother's hopes. Family legend has it that when he was five he announced, "One of these days I'm going to preach." However precocious, it was not an unlikely ambition. Jesse had heard from his mother that the Robinsons had produced a long line of Baptist ministers. Closer to home, his grandmother was the soul of religious devotion. Helen and Charles Jackson both sang in the church choir and had pictures of Jesus Christ on their walls and mantel.

At the age of nine, Jesse won a church election to the National Sunday School Convention, and once a month, at Sunday services, he spoke about the organization's business to the full congregation. To do so, he had to overcome both stage fright and a slight stutter in his speech.

"We developed a life-style built around the Bible," Jesse Jackson once said; for his stepfather, that meant his children were not only devout but hardworking. Jesse started working when he was six, picking up wood scraps in a lumberyard. From then on, before and after school and during the summer,

he worked at whatever jobs were open to a black youngster: hawking concessions at Furman games, shining shoes, ushering at a movie theater, caddying at the Greenville Country Club, and, by the time he was in high school, waiting on tables at the Poinsett Hotel.

Jesse's grandmother was not alone in thinking him special. "He stood head and shoulders above everybody at the age of six and could he talk," J. D. Mathis, his school coach, recalled. "I told him he was going to be heir apparent to great things."

On the white side of town, just about no one believed that Jesse or, for that matter, any black person was in the slightest way special. For the 60,000 residents of Greenville, white supremacy and segregation were facts of life, and as far as the whites were concerned, the sooner a youngster like Jesse learned it, the better. One day, he recalled later, "I went to catch a bus with my mother, and the sign above the bus driver's head said Colored Seat from the Rear. . . . My mother had to pull me to the back. I said I wanted to sit up front. She said, 'Let's go.' She pinched me."

Jackson (back row, third from right) stands next to his best friend, Owen Perkins (wearing dark tie), in a 1958 portrait of Sterling High's Camera Club. An honors student and sports star, Jackson also participated in almost every extracurricular activity his school offered.

Betty Davis, Sterling High's Miss Basketball of 1958, leaves her coronation ceremony on the arm of the school's tall, handsome basketball star, 17-year-old Jesse Jackson.

He risked more than a pinch by defying the customs of segregation. The corner grocery, a hangout for Jesse and his friends, was run by a white man named Jack. "We used to run in there and play with him, so I always thought of him as a friend," Jesse Jackson said.

One day, as shoppers crowded the aisles and Jack sliced bologna for a customer, Jesse rushed in. "Jack, I got to go right away and I got to have some candy," he shouted. Jack ignored him. Jesse repeated his demand. Again, no response. So Jesse whistled at the storekeeper. Jack dropped the bologna, reached under the counter for a .45 caliber revolver, and aimed it at Jesse's face. "Goddamn you," he screamed, "don't you ever whistle at me no more as long as you live." Everyone froze. "That store was full of black folks," Jesse recalled, "but not one of them moved and I didn't either."

Faced with Whites Only signs on theaters, restaurants, drinking fountains, and rest rooms, the blacks of Greenville did what they could to preserve a measure of dignity. "We would say we didn't want to drink water because we weren't thirsty," Jackson remembered, "or we didn't want to eat because we weren't hungry, or we didn't want to go to the movie theater because we didn't want to see the picture. Actually, we were lying because we were afraid."

They addressed the inequity of segregation in small ways—mocking the oppressive whites, for example. A schoolmate remembered how Jesse "used to make up jokes about whites, how foolish and stupid they were. He used to have me in stitches. He used to turn things around. The white and black football teams couldn't play together. And Jesse would always say, that's because they're scared they'd get whupped. Because the black team is better."

He was probably right about the football squads. Sterling High School, with Jesse Jackson playing quarterback, steamrollered nearly every team it played. "Jesse was the kind of kid you wanted as a quarterback," said his coach, "clean and an all-American type. He was big and he could take a punch and then dish out a blow."

Jesse was the picture of confidence when he took over as quarterback his junior year. Even the team's seniors, who were accustomed to pushing underclassmen around, respected him. In the huddle during one game, an older player, a wide receiver, said he doubted that Jesse could get the ball to him on a long fly pattern. "It'll be there—just make sure you are," Jesse snapped. And it was.

Unlike some other athletes, Jesse was as attentive to textbooks as he was to playbooks. "He was the only football player I ever had that asked for his assignment if he was going to miss class because of football practice," said a Sterling teacher. "The others would make excuses." It paid off. Jackson compiled an academic record so strong that, as a senior, he was chosen for the National Honor Society. "Growing up taught me to make A's; when you do people have to hang around you. With D's, they don't," he said.

But it was his athletic gifts that brought stadium crowds to their feet and that had girls, as Coach Mathis said, "falling all over themselves to get to Jesse." He heard the cheers year-round, playing not only football but basketball and baseball, too.

Every school has its all-around athlete. At Sterling it was Jesse Jackson. At Greenville High, the white school across town, Mr. Everything was Dickie Dietz. Sterling and Greenville, of course, never met on the field, but in pickup games, whites and blacks played ball together—until, as Jackson recalled, "the police would catch us and run us off." In these encounters, Jackson apparently got the best of Dietz. But for the local newspaper, it was all Dietz.

Jackson (25) offers a big smile in this 1959 yearbook shot of the Sterling High basketball team. The young athlete's skills attracted attention both on and off the court; according to Coach Mathis, the girls of Greenville "fell all over themselves to get to Jesse."

On the same night during one football season, Dietz kicked the extra point in a 7–6 win, while, at Sterling's Sirrine Stadium, Jackson had switched to halfback and scored all three of his team's touchdowns. The next day's paper headlined Dietz's heroic extra point. "Way down at the bottom of the page," Jesse remembered: "'Jackson makes three touchdowns. Sterling wins.' We lived with that kind of imbalance."

In the spring of 1959, a group of major league baseball scouts arrived in Greenville and invited the local talent to a tryout camp. Jackson and Dietz both showed up. A fireballing pitcher, Jesse had been striking out batters right and left, but it was Dietz, a slugging catcher, whom the scouts really wanted to see. "They asked me to pitch," Jackson said, "and guess who was doing the hitting? Dickie Dietz!"

For the first time in an organized competition, it was Jackson against Dietz, Sterling versus Greenville, black against white. Sitting together in the bleachers, several dozen blacks cheered themselves hoarse. "Yaaay, Jesse!" they screamed.

Dietz foul-tipped one pitch. That was it—the only wood he laid to one of Jackson's pitches. Three times the mighty Dietz struck out.

The blazing exhibition so impressed the scout for the San Francisco Giants that he offered Jackson a contract that carried a $6,000 signing bonus and an opportunity to play B-level ball in the minor leagues. That was quite a lot of money in 1959, twice what Jackson's stepfather earned in a year at the post office. Then Jackson discovered that the Giants had signed Dietz to a contract for A ball and handed him a bonus worth $95,000.

"I don't want this," Jackson informed the Giants.

He was going to college. "Six thousand seems big, but it can go fast," he explained years later. "I knew a college education would be less risk and greater return." ❧

3

"I ONLY WANT MY FREEDOM"

The biggest man on campus: Quarterback Jackson carries the ball for his alma mater, North Carolina Agricultural and Technical State University in Greensboro. Jackson was not only a football star but an honors student and president of the student body.

"HEY, NIGGER, OVER here!" the red-faced men in the bleachers at Textile Hall would shout. Jesse Jackson would haul over his vendor's tray of soft drinks, and somebody would give him a dollar, then want change for a ten. It was all in a night's work if you were black and sold concessions at the basketball games of Furman University.

Watching the games, Jackson dared to dream of a day when he would wear the purple and white of Furman, play on the court in Textile Hall, and, with his exploits, thrill the same fans who now yelled, "Hey, nigger, over here." He would show them.

It was not to be. Furman had never admitted a black and, in 1959, had no intention of doing so. However, in Bob King, a Furman coach, Jackson had a friend. Knowing of his desire to attend college and impressed by his athletic skills, King helped Jackson obtain a football scholarship to the University of Illinois. While the leading universities in Dixie stayed lily-white, the football powers of the Big Ten recruited talented southern blacks and were glad to have them on their rosters.

Jackson arrived in Champaign, Illinois, in the late summer of 1959. He expected to pick up where

39

he had left off in high school, calling the signals and
heaving touchdown passes, but a coach of the freshman team set him straight. Blacks were running
backs, linemen, and ends. "You people," the coach
kept saying. Dutifully, Jackson lined up at left halfback, then at left end. Inwardly he seethed. "It was
traumatic for me," he said, "black players being
reduced to entertainers."

Jackson was no happier away from the football
field. Set on a sprawling campus, with an enrollment
of 25,000 and a formidable academic reputation, the
university seemed remote, even hostile, to the newcomer from South Carolina. Blacks had long been
accepted as students, but seldom as equals. "We were
reduced to a subculture at Illinois," Jackson observed.
"The annual interfraternity dance was the social
event of the fall, only the black fraternities weren't
invited. My black friends and I were down at the
Veterans of Foreign Wars listening to 45s while the
white folks were jumping to Lionel Hampton in the
gym. Live."

Unhappy about what he had found in the integrated North, Jackson left Illinois after his freshman
year, not to return. In the fall of 1960, he enrolled at
North Carolina Agricultural and Technical State
University, a predominantly black state college in
Greensboro. "North Carolina A&T was my choice
because that was where the sit-ins started and it was
the students who started them," Jackson explained.

Eight months before Jackson's arrival in Greensboro, four North Carolina A&T freshmen, Ezell
Blair, Jr., Franklin McCain, Joe McNeil, and David
Richmond, had walked downtown and entered the
F. W. Woolworth store. When they reached the
lunch counter, they sat down. By so doing, they had
broken the law and custom of segregation. The
counter was for whites and whites only.

A black waitress had approached the young men.
"Fellows like you make our race look bad," she said,

North Carolina A&T students stage a sit-in at the whites-only lunch counter of a Greensboro variety store in 1960. Such courageous protests prompted Jesse Jackson to enter the largely black state college that fall.

and refused to serve them. The four smiled understandingly but remained in their seats and stayed there until the store closed. The next morning they were back, once more patiently waiting to be served. Nineteen more students had joined them. On the following day, February 3, a total of 85 students showed up. Organized by then, they began to sit in shifts of several hours each. The sit-in movement had been born.

The sit-ins raced across the upper South like wildfire. Over the following year, 50,000 students, white and black, all of them quietly determined to end segregation in eating places, took the simple, eloquent step of sitting down and waiting. They faced a barrage of hostility from whites, who screamed obscenities, poured condiments over them, and pressed lighted cigarettes into their skin.

But the demonstrations worked. By the end of 1961, rather than see their businesses hopelessly disrupted, store owners in 200 southern cities had desegregated their lunch counters. The peaceful protest, born on a North Carolina campus, had scored a significant victory in the American civil rights movement. Was it any wonder Jesse Jackson decided to enroll at North Carolina A&T?

A&T, which also had a football team, welcomed the refugee from Illinois. The team played on lumpy fields ringed by splintery wooden bleachers, light-years from the splendor of the Big Ten, but it did not matter to Jackson. At A&T he was the quarterback, calling the plays, running the show. An outcast at Illinois, he became the biggest man on campus in Greensboro—Saturday's hero, student body president, honor student, and second vice-grand basileus of Omega Psi Phi, his fraternity.

As in high school, Jackson had an eye for the young women in his vicinity and they for him. At first, though, his interest in Jacqueline Lavinia Davis, a 17-year-old freshman, was not romantic. Struggling with his term paper ("Should Red China Be Admitted to the United Nations?"), Jackson had approached Davis for some advice. After talking a while, she must have wondered why he was asking. Jesse "was a bit too fast, a bit too full of himself" to be interested in what anyone else had to say. "He didn't appeal to me initially," she said. "I was from a puritanical culture and I thought he was a little too quick in formulating opinions."

She would change her mind.

Born in Fort Pierce, Florida, in 1944, Jackie Davis came from a family of migrant farm workers. The oldest of five children, she never knew her father, but she had the protection and unbounded love of her mother, who supported her family by picking beans for 15 cents an hour. For a time, Davis considered becoming a nun, then decided on college and North Carolina A&T. In 1961, she was studying psychology and sociology.

Leaders of North Carolina A&T's sororities and fraternities gather for a campus conference in 1962. Standing third from the right is the second vice-grand basileus of Omega Psi Phi, aka Jesse Jackson.

Davis let no one wonder where she stood politically. Highly intelligent and intensely committed to the civil rights movement, she participated in demonstrations and was known on campus as a fiery champion of left-wing causes. She was also known as a beauty. An inch over five feet tall with a stunning figure, she possessed an air of absolute confidence.

Jackson found himself smitten. As he and Davis began seeing more of one another, what started as discussions of politics and world affairs turned to intimacy and laughter. Jackson was Davis's first boyfriend, and he was determined to be her last. On campus one day, to the delight of his friends, he shouted, "Hey, Jackie, you're going to marry me."

And she did. Sometime in 1962, she discovered she was pregnant. "I think Jesse did it to catch me," she speculated in 1987. "Because he kept asking me, 'Are you feeling sick?' A baby? I hadn't thought about a baby." In late 1962, they had a quiet wedding at Jackson's home in Greenville. "We got married and established family security. We broke the cycle," Jackson said, alluding to his and Davis's backgrounds of illegitimacy and single-parent households. On July 16, 1963, Jackie Jackson gave birth to their first child, a daughter they named Santita.

Although she dropped out of college to make a home and raise a family, Jackie Jackson retained her independence. "I did not marry my husband to imprison him," she once said. "Nor did he marry me to place me in a prison." Over the years, the Jackson marriage has been one of respect and equality. "He loves basketball," she once remarked, attempting to explain their relationship. "It doesn't make me happy to go and watch him play basketball. So, therefore, I love to swim. I think life is as simple as agreeing that you play basketball and I swim."

By 1963, Jesse Jackson had become the leader of student activism at A&T. With the same confidence he showed on the football field, he led columns of marchers from the campus to the local restaurants, theaters, and public buildings that barred or segregated blacks. Part of a southern campaign sponsored by the Congress of Racial Equality (CORE), the Greensboro protests proved, beyond any doubt, that Jesse Jackson was a man people followed.

On June 6, 1963, the demonstrators decided to intensify the protest, to deliberately court arrest, and to fill the jails with students whose only crime was demanding an end to segregation. That afternoon, Jackson, wearing a sharply pressed suit and a snap-brim hat, led several hundred demonstrators into downtown Greensboro. Reaching the intersection in front of the municipal building, they sat down and refused to budge. "I know I am going to jail," Jackson said to them. "I'm going without fear. It's a principle that I have. . . . I'll go to the chain gang if necessary."

With the students encamped on the street and traffic snarled for blocks, a police captain approached Jackson. "Now you've done it," he sputtered. "You're really messing up now." Jackson returned the captain's stare. Then, in a broad gesture, he pointed to the municipal building, headquarters of the city government that condoned and enforced segregation. "No," he said, "It's not me, Captain, they're the ones that are messing up."

The police moved in and arrested 278 of the demonstrators, including their leader, on charges of inciting a riot. Like nonviolent protesters before him, Jackson refused to post bond, preferring jail to any compromise with injustice. "I'm going to jail because I refuse to let another man put a timetable on

Detective William Jackson escorts activist college student Jesse Jackson to jail after arresting him for "inciting a riot"—actually, for organizing a peaceful protest against segregation—in June 1963. The two Jacksons, who crossed paths in numerous arrest situations, often engaged in philosophical discussions and eventually became good friends.

North Carolina A&T's president, Samuel Proctor, gives Jackson a hearty handshake and a medal for scholastic excellence in 1963. Proctor, who saw a fine potential clergyman in the 21-year-old South Carolinian, helped him get a scholarship at the Chicago Theological Seminary.

my freedom," he explained. "We aren't asking for integration. We're asking for desegregation and there's a difference. I only want my freedom."

When he left jail a few weeks later—the police dropped the charges—Jackson was a bigger man on campus than he had ever been before. Greensboro had caved in. Wanting peace and quiet rather than daily demonstrations, the city desegregated its downtown. Moreover, the national civil rights movement had taken notice of the tall young man from A&T. He became a field director for CORE, marked by the organization's director, James Farmer, as a rising star.

That summer, 21-year-old Jesse Jackson graduated from A&T with a degree in sociology. Before the commencement exercises, he had decided on his next step: a career in the ministry. He passed up a scholarship to Duke University Law School, and

with the counsel and assistance of A&T president
Samuel Proctor, secured a Rockefeller fellowship to
the Chicago Theological Seminary.

Jackson's decision had followed a period of considerable soul-searching. "One night he woke up and
said he had an odd dream," said his former A&T
roommate Charles Carter. "He said he thought he
had been called to preach. He was shaking. I never
saw him look so serious before."

The choice of the ministry was not altogether a
matter of midnight visions. As a boy, Jackson had
taken pride in the preachers who had cropped up in
every generation of the Robinson family. Later, his
enthusiasm for the ministry had cooled as he began to
look down on the fundamentalist, fire-and-brimstone
theology of the black church. "For a long time I
reacted negatively to the whole preaching thing," he
said, "because of my hang-up on traditional preaching and traditional preachers."

The civil rights movement restored his ambition.
It had been born in the black churches of the South
and its leaders were ministers. Jesse Jackson meant to
join them.

With his wife and daughter, Jackson moved to
Chicago and began his seminary studies in early
1964. "I really thought by going to seminary school it
would be quiet and peaceful and I could reflect," he
said. He described his days there as "precious," but in
the spring of 1965, six months before his graduation,
he dropped out of school and headed for Selma,
Alabama. There, in the heart of the old Confederacy,
Martin Luther King, Jr., was leading a crusade to
secure for southern blacks the most elemental right of
citizenship: the right to vote. ❦

4

A PATCH OF BLUE SKY

MARTIN LUTHER KING, JR., was the commanding moral force of his generation—the visionary leader of the civil rights movement. Beginning with the Montgomery bus boycott of 1955, King and the organization he founded, the Southern Christian Leadership Conference (SCLC), spearheaded a nonviolent revolution against segregation in the American South. The defenders of the old order, that of white supremacy, fought them every step of the way, answering the peaceful protests of the SCLC with jailings, clubbings, lynchings, and midnight bombings.

It was what King expected, even desired. The nation, he believed, had to see and understand the true nature of racial persecution. So, in 1963, on their television screens and in their newspapers, middle-class Americans witnessed the horror of Birmingham, Alabama, where King was thrown into solitary confinement at the city jail and where his disciples, many of them children, were mangled by police attack dogs and knocked senseless by high-pressure water hoses.

By 1965, as a result of the previous year's federal civil rights act, the Whites Only signs had come down in the restaurants, theaters, and hotels of Dixie. But they remained in place on the ballot boxes. King's last great effort in the South was directed against the fear and discrimination that kept southern blacks off the voting rolls. For their campaign, he and the SCLC selected Selma, Alabama, the seat of a county where 15,000 blacks were eligible to vote but only 325 did. "We are demanding the ballot," he cried.

On Sunday, March 7, 1965, 600 marchers, nearly all of them black, massed at Brown Chapel in Selma to begin a protest march to Montgomery, the state capital, 54 miles away. The protesters got as far as the Edmund Pettus Bridge on the edge of Selma. There, a phalanx of local and state policemen awaited them. In a few minutes, tear gas was clogging the air, and defenseless marchers were being clubbed by police in riot gear and trampled by a mounted posse brandishing cattle prods. It was a bloodbath.

That evening, along with film of the gruesome spectacle, network television ran an appeal from King to his fellow clergy. Come to Selma, he pleaded, we will march again.

In Chicago, Jesse Jackson watched the events of Bloody Sunday and knew he had no choice but to answer King's appeal. He went straight to Selma. When he got there, Jackson did not melt into the throng of marchers but broke for the front ranks. "I remembered getting a little annoyed," said Andrew Young, one of King's principal aides, "because Jesse was giving orders from the steps of Brown Chapel and nobody knew who he was. All the other marchers came up getting in line, but Jesse, assuming a staff role, automatically started directing the marchers."

Jackson, wearing a porkpie hat and denim work clothes, spoke in a voice that carried across the street. "I thought it strange that he would be making a speech," recalled Betty Washington, a correspondent for the Chicago *Daily Defender*, "when he was not on the SCLC staff and had not been included in any

of the strategy meetings. He just seemed to have come from nowhere. Like, who *was* he? But he spoke so well, I recorded his statement anyway. I had the feeling that one day he might be important."

Jackson's audacious behavior caught the notice of the Reverend Ralph Abernathy, King's right-hand man and closest friend. "There was something about him that impressed me," Abernathy said of Jackson. "I could see the leadership potential in him." When Jackson asked if there were any openings on the SCLC staff, Abernathy took it up with King.

King was skeptical. He "did not agree with me that we ought to employ this young man on the basis of my experience with him during that short time," Abernathy recalled. "Reluctantly he went along, though."

Martin Luther King, Jr. (front row, at right of flag), leads 10,000 civil rights marchers on the last leg of their monumental 54-mile trek from Selma, Alabama, to Montgomery in March 1965. Holding hands with King is his wife, Coretta; next to her is SCLC aide Hosea Williams. Other notable marchers are labor leader A. Philip Randolph (second from left), Ralph Abernathy (fourth from left), and diplomat Ralph Bunche (sixth from left).

It was Jackson's good luck that the SCLC was just then shifting its attention from South to North. Selma, for the time being, would be King's last effort in the South. The campaign there and the successful completion of the march to Montgomery helped ensure congressional approval of the Voting Rights Act of 1965. With the federal government stepping in to register and protect previously disfranchised southern blacks, the last pillar of legal segregation had fallen.

What now most troubled King was the plight of northern blacks. They had long had equality before the law, but all too often, they endured lives of crime, illness, and poverty in dilapidated inner-city slums. King meant to do something about it by bringing the SCLC north. He chose to begin in Chicago, Jackson's new hometown.

Placed on the SCLC payroll at $3,000 a year, Jackson was assigned to work under James Bevel in Chicago. Bevel liked the new recruit and carefully instructed him in the ways of nonviolent protest. Jackson was amazed at how much Bevel knew. "Bevel was the real creative genius of that period," he said later, "one of the most creative thinkers I've ever been exposed to." And, he might have added, one of the most colorful.

King tolerated, even appreciated, Bevel's lively nature. His skill as an organizer and eloquence as a speaker were too great to do otherwise. A newcomer such as Jackson soon found that free spirits such as Bevel fit right in at the SCLC. A staff member recalled that the "SCLC was a very rowdy place," and, he could have said, one chronically short of money and often in organizational disarray. But never, ever, was it lacking in purpose.

Its purpose in 1965 and 1966 was open housing in the nation's second city. Blacks constituted the largest ethnic group in Chicago, and nearly all of them lived in slums on the south and west sides of town. The rest of the city was white, and that was the way the white working-class residents wanted it to stay. "Most Chicago whites hated blacks," wrote local newspaperman Mike Royko. "The only genuine difference between a southern white and a Chicago white was in their accent."

Running Chicago was its red-faced, pudgy—and incomparably shrewd—mayor and political boss, Richard J. Daley. "Under Daley," wrote historian Theodore H. White, "ethnic municipal politics were to reach their classic triumph as an art form, as distinctively American as baseball." As long as they were loyal Democrats, Chicagoans could find a place in Daley's machine or on the city payroll. This was true not only for the Irish, Jews, Poles, and Czechs, but for blacks as well. However, as everyone knew, the upper rungs on the political ladder were painted white.

Jackson had been active in Democratic politics while he was at A&T, campaigning for North Carolina's Democratic governor, Terry Sanford. To show his appreciation, Sanford gave his young supporter a letter of introduction to Daley. Shortly after he returned to Chicago, Jackson called on Daley and presented the letter. The mayor looked it up and down. "See your ward committeeman," he said. Daley was suggesting that if Jackson pounded the pavement of his precinct for a few elections and proved he could turn out the vote, then, perhaps, some job for him might be found. Something like— the mayor thought for a moment—coin collector on one of the city toll roads.

Jackson had called on Daley to establish a working relationship with city hall, not because he wanted a job. He was committed to the battle for civil rights and had no intention of leaving the SCLC. Thousands of Chicago blacks, however, would have

SCLC official James Bevel speaks at a black Chicago church in the mid-1960s. Once a successful rock and roll performer, Bevel had experienced a religious conversion and become a Baptist clergyman. By the time Jackson went to work for him in 1965, he was a veteran civil rights activist.

In 1965, when Chicago mayor Richard J. Daley (opposite page) met Jackson (above) for the first time, the old political boss regarded the young black activist as nothing more than an eager job seeker. In the years to come, Daley would learn he had made a serious misjudgment.

jumped at Daley's suggestion. It was through such patronage and favors that the Daley machine controlled the black vote and, for a long while, black behavior in Chicago. Black community leaders, particularly in the older, established South Side, were Daley's people. "Negro ministers may think they're servants of God, but they're servants of Daley—or maybe that's the same thing," joked one black politician.

"We entered a different world when we came to this northern city in 1966, a world we didn't fully understand," wrote Ralph Abernathy of the SCLC in Chicago. Driving a borrowed Cadillac, Jackson showed King and Abernathy around. The two ministers expressed amazement at the size of the city's sprawling South Side. "That's nothing," said Jackson. "Wait till you see the West Side." He took them there. Abernathy remembered "looking over at Martin and both of us shaking our heads. The number of people living in the squalid devastation was beyond our comprehension."

The public phase of the SCLC's Chicago campaign got under way on July 10, 1966—Freedom Sunday—with a lakefront rally at Soldier Field followed by a King-led march to City Hall. On Monday morning, King and 11 colleagues, including Jackson, met with Daley. The mayor pledged cooperation (although nothing too specific) and said that he too hated slums and was going to clean them up.

Keep stalling and maybe King will go away, seemed to be Daley's strategy, and so far, it seemed to be working. But at the Monday morning meeting, Al Raby, a local activist who had begun the Chicago open-housing movement and who had invited King to town in the first place, looked Daley straight in the eye. "I want you to know we are going to begin direct action, immediately," Raby said bluntly. Daley, who had a short fuse, lost his temper, and the meeting wound up as a shouting match.

Daley was angry because he was worried. By direct action, Raby meant that blacks from the inner city planned to march into the white blue-collar neighborhoods that excluded them. Such a move would pit two groups of Daley's staunchest supporters—blacks and white ethnics—against one another, a confrontation that could mean nothing but bad news to the mayor.

On the evening of July 29, a group of 50 protesters arrived in the all-white Gage Park neighborhood and settled down in front of the offices of the Halvorsen Realty Company. The demonstration's leaders—Jackson, Bevel, and Raby—announced that they would stay there all night to protest the firm's policies of discriminating against blacks. By 9 o'clock, more than 1,000 enraged whites had descended on the demonstrators. Although several dozen policemen strained to keep them back, the whites got close enough to shower the visitors with debris and racial epithets. The demonstrators retreated.

The next day, their number swollen to 500, the demonstrators returned to the Halvorsen office in Gage Park. This time, bottles and bricks hit both Jackson and Raby. On Sunday, Raby led a car caravan into Marquette Park, another all-white community. Before the day was over, 15 of the demonstrators' cars, all of them unoccupied, had been overturned and set afire.

On August 5, King himself led a procession into Marquette Park. Its residents greeted the 1964 winner of the Nobel Peace Prize with a hail of stones and broken glass. A rock struck King on the side of his head and he sank to one knee. "I would never forget the look in the eyes of this man who had survived Birmingham and Montgomery and Selma," wrote *Time* correspondent Robert Sam Anson. "It was of sheer terror." Although he was not badly hurt, King was appalled by the ferocity of northern whites. "I think the people from Mississippi ought to come to Chicago to learn how to hate," he said.

The marches continued. On Sunday, August 7, Jackson directed 2,000 protesters into the Belmont-Cregin neighborhood. When they stopped marching to kneel in prayer, they heard the neighborhood whites singing a familiar tune, an advertising jingle for a brand of frankfurters. Its lyrics, though, had been changed:

> I wish I were an Alabama trooper,
> That is what I would truly like to be:
> I wish I were an Alabama trooper
> 'Cause then I could kill the niggers legally.

The following day, with King out of town, Jackson announced the next target of the protest: Cicero, the tightly packed suburb just across Chicago's western city limit. The plan sent a shudder through nearly everyone who heard about it. Cicero promised to be not only the protest's next stop but its last.

A community of 70,000 people, every one of them white, Cicero held 2 claims to fame: During the 1920s, it had cheerfully welcomed the gangster Al Capone; and in 1951, when a black family purchased a house there, 4,000 whites had started a riot that ended only with the dispatch of the National Guard. "We expect violence," Jackson admitted. No one disagreed. "Jesus, they won't make it," said a Cicero politician. "If they get in, they won't get out."

Jackson's announcement caught the SCLC and the Chicago organizers off balance. The protest leaders had discussed going to Cicero but had reached no decision. King, away on SCLC business in Mississippi, was "a little angry," Abernathy recalled. "He had not wanted to tip off our future plans and . . . our demoralized army did not want to hear about even more difficult battlegrounds at a time when they were encountering enough trouble in Gage Park and Marquette Park."

To some of his colleagues in Chicago, Jackson had become a show horse, one no longer willing to pull with the team. "Jesse would often make major policy statements without clearing them with anyone," said Don Rose, a Chicago organizer. "The march announcement came one night when the cameras were on him. He couldn't resist saying something sensational."

King, too, had begun to speculate about Jackson's motives: Was he interested in the movement or in himself? Bevel often stood up for his friend when King questioned his devotion. "He's crude 'cause he's young," Bevel would say.

"No, he's ambitious," King would reply.

But no matter what the SCLC inner circle thought of Jackson, the organization stood behind his pledge of a march to Cicero and tentatively scheduled it for late August. Meanwhile, protests in other all-white neighborhoods kept on. It was too much for Mayor Daley. Marches day after day, combined with the specter of a racial holocaust in Cicero, brought him if not to his knees at least to the conference table.

After a series of meetings, Daley and the SCLC leaders reached an agreement on August 26: The city of Chicago would enforce the open-housing laws, and from then on, realtors would be compelled to stop discriminating against blacks.

King was ecstatic. Canceling plans for future Chicago-area marches, he announced that "the total eradication of housing discrimination has been made possible." Others, however, were not so sure. "I don't know," said Bevel when asked about the pact. "I'll have to think about it."

Bevel's doubts were well founded. As things turned out, Daley and his administration gave the agreement lip service but little else. The mayor had succeeded in stopping the marches and in getting King out of town. With that, his interest in open

Martin Luther King, Jr. (left), kneels in prayer with other SCLC members before beginning a civil rights demonstration. Although they were often beaten, jailed, and vilified by racist whites, King and his followers maintained a firm policy of nonviolence throughout their campaign.

housing quickly evaporated. A generation later, Chicago still possessed the most racially segregated housing patterns of any large American city.

Realizing he had been outmaneuvered, King attempted to turn Chicago blacks against their mayor; in late 1966, the SCLC launched a voter-registration drive. King might as well have decided to go 15 rounds with Muhammad Ali. When it came to registering voters and counting their ballots, Daley was the undisputed heavyweight champion. The SCLC got nowhere. In April 1967, Daley cruised to reelection for a fourth term, in the process capturing 73 percent of the total vote and a staggering 83 percent of the black vote.

In the midst of the storms over open housing and voter registration, there appeared a patch of blue sky for the SCLC, and it was largely Jackson's doing.

When Bevel had arrived in Chicago to set up an SCLC office, he brought along plans to implement Operation Breadbasket, the organization's economic arm. Founded in Philadelphia by the Reverend Leon Sullivan, transplanted to Atlanta and the SCLC in 1962, Breadbasket aimed to expand black employment at companies whose products blacks bought. If a company refused to hire more blacks, or if it discriminated against its existing black employees, then black consumers, organized by their ministers, would boycott the firm. Breadbasket also sought to encourage white-controlled businesses to invest in black-owned banks and companies.

Breadbasket appealed to Jackson, who found it particularly valuable in Chicago. With so many black preachers in the grip of the Daley machine, church endorsements of the open-housing campaign were few and far between. "It was clear that the ministers preferred a separate, but related program to the movement," Jackson recalled. Placed in charge of the Chicago operation by King in November 1965,

Jackson recruited more than 200 ministers to its banner within a few months.

The Breadbasket strategy was straightforward. First, identify firms that did business in black neighborhoods but that employed few blacks. Second, approach the company's executives and request they mend their ways. If that failed, begin picketing the company's retail outlets and encourage black consumers to take their trade elsewhere. A consumer boycott was a powerful weapon. "We are the margin of profit of every major item produced in America from General Motors cars on down to Kellogg's Corn Flakes," Jackson said.

Breadbasket first targeted Country's Delight Dairy, a company with no black drivers or sales representatives. At their first meeting, the dairy's executives told the Breadbasket ministers, in so many

Jackson and Ralph Abernathy exchange a hug before going into action at a Washington, D.C., protest march in the late 1960s. One of the first members of the civil rights movement to spot Jackson as a natural leader, Abernathy called him "a genius at motivating people."

words, to get lost. Within days, picket lines appeared in front of stores carrying Country's Delight products, and black consumers were buying other brands. After a week of seeing their milk sour in the groceries, dairy executives had a sudden change of heart. Within 30 days, a company spokesman announced, the dairy would hire 44 new black workers.

Strengthened by success, Operation Breadbasket swept through the rest of the dairy business in Chicago. By the end of the summer of 1966, 3 more dairies had agreed to provide blacks with 119 new jobs. "You can't beat them," groused a dairy boss. "They got that weapon and you have to respect it. If you don't you can go broke."

In August, Breadbasket began a boycott of Pepsi. Caving in quickly, Pepsico, Inc., came up with 32 new jobs. The bottlers of Coca-Cola, 7-Up, and Canfield surrendered without a fight, together promising 100 openings for blacks.

King was impressed with Breadbasket's achievements, particularly when he contrasted them with the dismal open-housing and voter-registration drives in Chicago. Jackson's stock rose. King doubled his SCLC salary, to $6,000 a year, and in early 1967 gave him control of the entire Operation Breadbasket program. Jackson responded by drafting strategies for expanding Breadbasket into other cities and into other fields, particularly those involved with helping black-owned businesses.

Jackson's relationship with King had its ups and downs. During 1967, it headed downward as King found it increasingly difficult to control his subordinate's activities. Jackson stayed in Chicago, preferring to run Operation Breadbasket from there rather than moving to SCLC headquarters in Atlanta, where he might have been monitored more closely. William Rutherford, the SCLC executive director, remembered King saying to him, "Jesse Jackson's so independent, I either want him in SCLC or out—you go whichever way you want to, but one way or the other, he's a part of SCLC or he's not a part of SCLC."

Sometimes it seemed Jackson just rubbed King the wrong way. "Martin had problems with Jesse because Jesse would ask questions," one associate said. He also tended to argue and press his case long past the point of accomplishing anything other than irritating King. King's interests in 1967 and early 1968 focused on opposing American involvement in Vietnam and organizing the Poor People's March on Washington. The more he concentrated on these projects, the less he wanted to hear about Operation Breadbasket.

And the less patience he had for arguing with Jackson. On a Saturday in late March 1968, during an exhausting, contentious SCLC meeting in Atlanta, Jackson made no attempt to hide his scorn for some of King's plans. Others did the same. King could take no more of it and abruptly got up to leave. Jackson rose and followed him to the door. King stopped in his tracks, spun around, and snapped, "If you are so interested in doing your own thing that you can't do what the organization is structured to do, go ahead. If you want to carve out your own niche in society, go ahead, but for God's sake don't bother me!"

Four days later, King left Atlanta to offer his help to some striking sanitation workers in Memphis, Tennessee. ❧

5

THE HEIR APPARENT

———— ❦ ————

THERE WAS A chill in the early evening air in Memphis, and the driver of the white Cadillac limousine called up to Martin Luther King, Jr., waiting on the second-floor balcony of the Lorraine Motel, and said he had best bring a topcoat. "O.K.," came the reply.

Down in the motel courtyard, gathered around the Cadillac, killing time until they all got into the big car and went to dinner, were five of King's lieutenants: Andrew Young, James Bevel, Chauncey Eskridge, Hosea Williams, and, in a brown turtleneck shirt, brown trousers, and brown shoes, Jesse Jackson.

Jackson's mood also might well have been brown. He had come to Memphis with the others to organize a march on behalf of the striking garbage collectors, but his relations with King were chillier than the evening air. Far from regretting the tongue-lashing he had given Jackson the previous week in Atlanta, King had repeated it the night before. "Jesse, just leave me alone," he had said. "Go any place you want to, do anything you want to do, but leave me alone."

Martin Luther King, Jr. (center), and his aides Jackson and Ralph Abernathy gather on the balcony of the Lorraine Motel shortly after their arrival in Memphis, Tennessee, on April 3, 1968. Standing at the same spot the next day, King fell to the bullets of assassin James Earl Ray, an escaped white convict who later confessed to the murder and received a 99-year prison sentence.

There was no place Jackson wanted to go. "Don't send me away," he had begged King.

But on the balcony that evening, seeing Jackson downstairs by the white car, King had said to him, loud enough for everyone to hear: "I want you to come to dinner with me." Could it be the sign he was back in King's good graces?

Jackson smiled and took the moment to introduce Ben Branch, a musician who played for Operation Breadbasket in Chicago and who would be performing at a rally for the Memphis strikers that evening. "Ben, make sure you play 'Precious Lord, Take My Hand' at the meeting tonight," King said, leaning forward as he talked, placing both hands on the balcony railing. "Sing it real pretty."

It was one minute past six on April 4, 1968. King had not yet moved to fetch his topcoat. Ralph Abernathy was inside the room, number 306, that he shared with King, splashing on some of his roommate's Aramis aftershave lotion.

There came a muffled explosion, the kind that sounds like a car backfiring or a firecracker going off. The men around the Cadillac instinctively ducked for cover. Abernathy turned and through the open door of room 306 saw King's body sprawled on the balcony. He rushed out and found his friend lying in a spreading pool of blood. The right side of his jaw had been blown away.

"Martin, Martin, this is Ralph. Do you hear me? This is Ralph." King's lips moved, but no words came. An hour later, at five minutes past seven, he was pronounced dead. He was 39 years old.

The assassination of Martin Luther King, Jr., was a national tragedy. As soon as the bulletins of the shooting flashed onto radio and television, agonized and enraged blacks stormed into the streets. Over the next several days, rioting scarred and, in some cases, demolished the black neighborhoods of 126 cities.

Thirty-nine people died in the arson, looting, and gunfire. The carnage seemed a horrible negation of King's philosophy and legacy of nonviolence.

For Jackson, the assassination was a personal tragedy. King was his idol and inspiration, his mentor and moral conscience. Nevertheless, what his SCLC colleagues saw in the hours following the murder was not the picture of a grief-stricken disciple.

By every account of the shooting, Ralph Abernathy was the first to reach King. Then came Andrew Young, who raced upstairs from the court-yard. Following Young was James Laue, an observer from the Department of Justice occupying a nearby room, who placed a folded towel under King's bleeding head. Abernathy held his dying friend in his arms and on his lap. At six minutes past six, an ambulance arrived.

A mule-drawn caisson carries King's coffin through the streets of Atlanta. Among those accompanying the fallen leader are Jackson (last row, second from the left) and, at left rear of coffin, SCLC executive vice-president Andrew Young.

Hosea Williams recalled that after Jackson went up the staircase, "He just stood there. Then, I think he ran for a phone to call Coretta." In Atlanta, Coretta Scott King had just returned home from shopping. Jackson informed her of the shooting, advised her to come to Memphis, and to soften the news, said her husband had been wounded in the shoulder.

At 6:25, camera crews from the television networks started arriving. "Don't talk to them," Jackson ordered the other SCLC staffers. Minutes later, said Williams, "I was in my room. I looked out and saw Jesse talking to these TV people. . . . I heard Jesse say, 'Yes, I was the last man in the world King spoke to.' "

Jackson flew to Chicago later that evening. Early the next morning, after what had been a virtually sleepless night, several SCLC staff members mustered in a room at the Lorraine. The television, its volume low, was tuned to NBC's "Today Show." "Somebody called me," Williams said, "'Come quick, look who's on TV.' " It was Jackson, wearing the brown turtleneck from the night before. It was smeared with blood. To the amazement of his comrades in Memphis, Jackson was saying it was the blood of Martin Luther King, Jr., and that it had gotten there when he cradled the fallen leader in his arms.

The media picked up and held on to Jackson's version of the assassination: "Jesse ran to the balcony, held King's head, but it was too late," reported *Time*. The press also accepted Jackson's claim to the top: In 1969, *Playboy* called him "King's heir apparent."

There was, however, a question of precisely how much King's legacy was worth. During the last few years of his life, King had lost considerable standing in black America. His principles of nonviolence and integration had come under assault from all directions. The Black Muslims preached black separatism. Stokely Carmichael and H. Rap Brown promoted

Black Power. The Black Panthers embraced Marxist ideology and armed themselves for what they said was an inevitable war with whites. These black militants drew their greatest strength in the ghettos of northern cities, the very places where, as his failures in Chicago had shown, King was his weakest.

Jackson meant to succeed where King had failed. "Jesse was probably the only one . . . who could attract the urban young and still work on the program of nonviolence," said a Chicago associate. "It was an effort to update the spirit of Dr. King in the northern urban context, an effort to get kids who seemed to be going off in another direction."

Ralph Abernathy took over the leadership of the SCLC. Jackson's vehicle would be Operation Breadbasket; his message, black economic power.

Jackson's manner was in direct contrast to King's. A product of Atlanta's black aristocracy, King had projected an image of probity, carefully dressed in a somber suit, white shirt, and a skinny tie held motionless by a pearl tiepin. If he changed clothes for a protest, he put on the raiment of the rural poor: bib overalls, a denim shirt, and rough work boots.

The young blacks in the ghettos of Chicago and New York and Cleveland plainly did not emulate men who dressed like that, like accountants or sharecroppers. They dressed as Jackson did, in striped vests and bell-bottom trousers, in dashikis, leather coats, gold medallions, and, in what became a symbol, sneakers. "I'm a man of the streets, not of the office," Jackson said. When the Chicago Theological Seminary awarded him an honorary degree in 1968, he accepted it wearing the traditional cap and gown. Then, for all to see, he removed the robe to reveal Levi's and a turtleneck.

Operation Breadbasket survived on Jackson's speeches. Without Jackson to whip up support, there would have been no picket lines, no boycotts, no educated consumers. Every Saturday morning in

Newly named an honorary doctor of divinity by Chicago Theological Seminary, Jackson reveals his standard outfit of turtleneck shirt and jeans beneath his academic robe. Moments after the June 1969 award ceremony ended, Jackson went back to leading a hunger-protest march from Chicago to Springfield, the Illinois capital.

Reporters, photographers, policemen, and protesters listen as Jackson, speaking outside the governor's mansion in Indianapolis, Indiana, in July 1969, demands the hiring of more black state workers. Jackson's fiery, energetic leadership of Operation Breadbasket, which attempted to expand black employment at companies whose products blacks bought, made the SCLC organization a smashing success.

Chicago's Capitol Theater, Jackson presided over a Breadbasket rally, an affair that was equal parts church service, political rally, lecture, and concert. Before he rose to deliver his message of pride and economic self-help, the Breadbasket choir and a 13-piece jazz band would bring the audience to a state of hand-clapping, body-swaying excitement with up-tempo versions of old standard hymns. Then Jackson, tall and handsome, would step to the pulpit and say, "Good morning, brothers and sisters. Repeat after me":

> I am—Somebody!
> I may be poor, but I am—Somebody!
> I may be on welfare but I am—Somebody!
> I may be uneducated, but I am—Somebody!
> I may be in jail, but I am—Somebody!
> I am—Somebody!
> I must be, I'm God's child.
> I must be respected and protected.
> I am black and I am beautiful!
> I am—Somebody!
> SOUL POWER!!!

After each line, he paused and the devoted audience repeated his words.

Jackson stressed the necessity of blacks patronizing black businesses: "Rather than looking through the Yellow Pages we have to start looking through the black pages. The trouble is that Negroes have been programmed by white folks to believe their products are inferior. We've developed a generation of Oreos—black on the outside, white on the inside."

It was a riveting performance, one he repeated countless times in countless places. "Nobody could do more with a crowd of potential supporters waiting to be told what to do," wrote Abernathy. "He instinctively knew their hearts, and he was a master of the right phrase to bring out their passion. When he spoke to such crowds he always quickened their blood."

Jackson carried his appeal across the country, traveling constantly, inspiring the young urban blacks who heard him. They listened to Jackson with something approaching awe as he explained the tactics of protest: "Turn on the pressure and don't ever turn it off. Don't forget one thing: When you turn on the gas you gotta cook or burn 'em up."

The country preacher, as he had taken to calling himself, enraptured the national media as well. Jackson, in Abernathy's words, "could promote a press conference on the smallest pretext and end up the lead story on the evening news." Within the space of five months in late 1969 and early 1970, Jackson received two of the garlands of American celebrity: an interview in *Playboy* and a front-cover story in *Time*.

He had less success in transforming Operation Breadbasket from a local to a national organization. During 1967 and 1968, he had led a highly effective boycott against A&P supermarkets in Chicago. Attempting the same thing in other cities, however, proved tough going. Jackson staged several protests at A&P's headquarters in New York City (getting arrested for one in 1971), but the firm resisted all his pressure. Other efforts at a nationwide campaign also fizzled. "The main problem with Breadbasket," wrote Abernathy, "was that it never existed outside of Chicago, except on paper; and even the paper organization was sketchy and full of holes."

Jackson's growing fame was coupled with a growing family. On March 11, 1965, soon after he arrived in Selma to join the voting rights protest, he got the news of the birth of his second child, Jesse Louis Jackson, Jr. In early 1966, Jackie Jackson gave birth to another boy, whom the couple named Jonathan Luther. He was followed by a third son, Yusef Dubois, in 1970, and in September 1975, by a daughter, Jacqueline Lavinia. Growing up, the children sometimes saw their peripatetic father only a few days a month; it fell to Jackie Jackson to run the house and raise the children.

In 1970, the Jacksons moved into a 15-room Tudor-style stucco house on tree-lined Constance Avenue, a few blocks from Lake Michigan in a pleasant, integrated neighborhood on Chicago's South Side. With Jesse home, the house was the scene of constant movement. To the front door trooped the official visitors—the press, out-of-town politicians, and business leaders. They were greeted and entertained in the front parlor, a room furnished with leather couches and velvet curtains. Friends and close associates used the back door and gathered in the dining room, a cheerful space that also housed some of Jackie's half-refinished antiques and Jesse's seldom-used golf clubs.

Among the callers was Jackson's half brother, Noah Robinson, Jr. Needing someone to run the business end of Breadbasket, Jackson had selected his half brother, now a graduate of Philadelphia's prestigious Wharton School of Finance and Commerce. Things had changed dramatically since Greenville. Once the outsider, it was Jesse whose picture was on the cover of *Time*, Jesse who could dazzle Noah by taking him to dinner with Diana Ross.

"I wanted to help him and please my father as well," Jackson said of his reasons for hiring his half brother. He placed Robinson at the head of the Breadbasket Commercial Association (BCA), a new agency charged with helping black businesses secure contracts from white-owned firms. With Robinson calling the shots, the BCA got off to a fast start; in the first half of 1970, it secured $16 million worth of contracts for black companies.

Unfortunately, Robinson seemed to view Breadbasket not only as a social service organization but as a means to personal profit. The half brothers' partnership lasted less than a year. In late 1970, Jackson fired Robinson, but when Robinson left, he took the BCA with him. Using its name, he went right on brokering contracts and soon became a construction subcontractor himself. Because the law required a certain amount of the work on federally funded projects to be set aside for minority contractors, Robinson had a very good thing going. "I wasn't ashamed of making millions," he said. As for his relations with Jackson after their blowup in 1970: "We didn't speak to each other for five years," said Robinson.

Jackson's relationship with Ralph Abernathy was deteriorating, too. Abernathy's tenure as SCLC chief was not a happy one. "Martin Luther King *was* the SCLC," said one associate, suggesting that no successor would have had an easy time. Abernathy, though, did a particularly bad job of it. Under his ineffective leadership, members left and contributions dried up. Jackson, theoretically a subordinate, won the lion's share of media attention, consolidated more and more power in Chicago, and displayed open contempt for Abernathy.

At the end of each year, the SCLC required Breadbasket to present a complete, orderly accounting of its finances. "What we got from Chicago was little more than a paper bag full of canceled checks

Recently suspended from a Boston high school for wearing his dashiki (a loose-fitting, African-style shirt) to class, Glen Grayson (second from left) discusses the clothing issue with friends. Black teenagers all over the country found they could relate to Jackson, whose sharp dress style reflected their own tastes.

and receipts—and more of the former than the latter," Abernathy recalled.

The relationship between the two men worsened steadily until, in late 1971, it exploded. The immediate cause was Jackson's handling of Black Expo, a yearly celebration and trade fair sponsored by Operation Breadbasket. Begun in 1969, Black Expo offered an opportunity for black companies to display their wares; for black leaders to state their cases; for writers, entertainers, athletes, and scholars to encourage black pride. A smashing success, it attracted huge crowds; tens of thousands descended on Chicago's International Amphitheater and paid their admission to see Expo's attractions.

It was Jackson's show. At the 1970 Expo, all mention of Abernathy was dropped from the exhibits even though the SCLC, as Breadbasket's parent, was the official sponsor. In 1971, Jackson went a step further, secretly incorporating Expo under its own charter and thereby severing its tie with the SCLC.

Fighting back, Abernathy ordered an audit of Black Expo's books. At about the same time, the *Chicago Tribune* began digging into the same field. Both the accountants and the reporters discovered a serious discrepancy: The gate receipts for Expo did not match the number of people attending. Unaccounted for was a sum somewhere between $100,000 and $400,000.

Jackson had generally steered clear of Expo's financial affairs, but as the fair's organizer, he was responsible for any financial discrepancies. On December 3, 1971, a typically snowy Chicago day, Abernathy and the SCLC board came to town and convened at a hotel near Chicago-O'Hare International Airport to decide Jackson's fate.

Marching outside in the snow, several picketers carried signs with a message for Abernathy: "Don't Get Messy with Jesse." Inside, the SCLC chief and his board met in a conference room and went over

Jackson leaves the Chicago conference room where, on December 3, 1971, he received a 60-day suspension from the SCLC for an accounting discrepancy involving Operation Breadbasket. Fuming at the reprimand, Jackson waited only nine days before announcing his resignation from the SCLC and his establishment of a new organization, PUSH, which now stands for People United to Serve Humanity.

the books. Several times Jackson tried to join them. "We are not ready to see you now," Abernathy scolded. "Wait until you're called." After three hours, he at last summoned Jackson. The board had decided to suspend him, with pay, from all SCLC activities for 60 days. After that, Jackson could resume his place as the head of Operation Breadbasket.

It amounted to a mere slap on the wrist, but Jackson was having none of it. On December 12, 1971, he announced his resignation from the SCLC. To his followers in Chicago he said, "I love the organization that I grew up with. . . . But I need air. I got to grow." ✿

THE D... AGAINST...

THESE MEN ARE DANGEROUS... THEY ARE CONSPIRING TO
CHILDREN, DESTROY FAMILIES, FORCE WOMEN INTO SLAVERY AND EXPLOIT
POOR PEOPLE - ALL IN THE NAME OF "WELFARE REFORM"

STOP THESE MEN!
H.R.1 must be stopped. Join NWRO in supporting
the Children's March for Survival - March 25 Wash. D.C.
NATIONAL WELFARE RIGHTS ORGANIZATION

6

OPERATION PUSH

O N DECEMBER 12, 1971, the very day Jackson sent a telegram of resignation to Abernathy, an imposing group of black Americans assembled in a suite of the old Commodore Hotel, next door to New York City's Grand Central Terminal. Some—singers Roberta Flack and Aretha Franklin, for example—were instantly recognized celebrities. Others—such as Carl Stokes, former mayor of Cleveland, Ohio, and Richard Hatcher, mayor of Gary, Indiana—were political wheelhorses. Al Johnson, a Chicago Cadillac dealer, was anonymous but rich. Ed Lewis and Clarence Jones, of *Essence* magazine and the *Amsterdam News* respectively, represented the black press. Junius Griffin of Motown Records represented himself and a large bank account.

These people, who had assembled at Jackson's invitation, laid the groundwork for a new organization, one crafted to supplant Operation Breadbasket. They would help finance it, and Jackson would run it. "We don't care what you call the movement as long as you stay the same," an admiring businessman told Jackson.

Less than two weeks later, on Christmas Day 1971, Jackson was in Chicago to unveil the new movement, Operation PUSH (People United to Save Humanity). "A new child has been born," he proclaimed.

With George Wiley (right) of the National Welfare Rights Organization, Jackson directs participants in the Children's March for Survival, a 1972 demonstration held in Washington, D.C.

The nation's first black congresswoman, Shirley Chisholm of New York, announces her support of Democratic presidential candidate George McGovern in July 1972. Chisholm had sought the nomination herself but gave up when she realized she had little backing from the black male politicians of her party.

To some extent, PUSH was old wine in a new bottle. Most of Operation Breadbasket's staff owed their jobs and loyalty to Jackson and came to PUSH with him. The same was true for the allegiances of the Chicago ministers who had backed Breadbasket's various campaigns. In the way of objectives, PUSH borrowed Breadbasket's goal of black economic growth: new jobs, companies, and products.

Yet PUSH, which eventually changed its name to People United to *Serve* Humanity, was different from Breadbasket. In the first place, Jackson was altogether on his own. There was no SCLC, no Ralph Abernathy looking over his shoulder. PUSH also had a clear political purpose. King and Abernathy had kept the SCLC out of electoral politics, but as stated in its initial prospectus, PUSH aimed "to elect to local, state, and federal office persons committed to human, economic, and social programs."

Richard J. Daley did not strictly fit that description. For some time, Jackson had been gunning for him, and in early 1971, as Daley launched his bid for a fifth term, Jackson had proposed himself as a candidate for mayor. When Jackson supporters failed to come up with enough petition signatures to place his name on the ballot, he announced he would run as a write-in candidate. Giving up on that tactic at the last minute, he finally endorsed Richard Friedman, a liberal Democrat who had the solid support of Chicago's reformers. On election day, Daley rolled to another 4 years in City Hall with 71 percent of the vote. For his part in the struggle against the mayor, Jackson collected 35 write-in votes.

Thirty-five votes! In the dining rooms and corridors of the LaSalle Hotel, stamping grounds for Chicago's regular Democrats, the Daley men had themselves a long, loud laugh. For six years, Jackson had been a thorn in their sides. His activism and appeal had threatened to undercut the machine in the city's black wards. But now, they roared, when it really counted, on election day, the "country preacher" drew a miserable 35 votes.

A year later, the hilarity had long since died, because by then Jackson had beaten the old pros at their own game.

"See Dick Daley." For years, every Democrat thinking of running for president had heard and taken that advice. As boss of Chicago, Daley also bossed the big Illinois delegation to the Democratic National Convention, and at the four conventions from 1956 to 1968 he had delivered the delegation's bloc of votes to the winning candidate. The 1972 convention promised to be no different.

Meanwhile, Jackson had been doing his level best to make it a very different sort of election year. During the fall of 1971, he tried to get off the ground a black political party. He suggested Representative John Conyers of Michigan as its presidential candidate. The plan never flew. The Congressional Black Caucus, a recently formed organization of blacks in Congress, adamantly opposed the idea.

There already was a black candidate in the race: Representative Shirley Chisholm of New York was seeking the Democratic nomination. But she received little support from most black leaders. Jackson, for one, never seriously considered backing Chisholm. Instead, he endorsed Senator George S. McGovern of South Dakota, the most liberal candidate in the field. A passionate opponent of the Vietnam War, McGovern was in charge of a full-scale revolt within the Democratic party. In his ranks were the young antiwar protesters, feminists, environmentalists, welfare rights activists, and, after April 1972, Jesse Jackson.

McGovern presented Jackson with an opportunity to even some scores with Daley. A clause in the

Democratic party's newly adopted charter (written a few years earlier by a commission cochaired by McGovern himself) required each delegation to the convention to include blacks, women, and young people in a number precisely proportionate to their numbers in the general population. The 59 delegates, handpicked by Daley and elected in March, were, unsurprisingly, mostly white, male, and old. "I don't give a damn about the McGovern rules," snorted the mayor.

Joining with Chicago alderman William Singer, Jackson demanded that the party unseat the 59 delegates loyal to Daley because the delegation clearly violated the new rules. Jackson and Singer orchestrated a hurried selection of an alternative 59 delegates, most of them young, more than half of them women, a third of them black, one of them Jesse Jackson. Daley responded with characteristic directness: He tried—unsuccessfully, as it turned out—to have Singer arrested.

Which delegation would it be, Daley's or the Jackson-Singer slate? The decision would be made by a credentials committee and then voted on by the full convention. At the last minute, Jackson proposed a compromise: Seat both delegations, and give half-votes to each side. Daley was in no mood for a deal. For the mayor, who had been attending Democratic conventions since before Jackson was born, it was to be all or nothing.

It was nothing. Meeting in Miami Beach, the convention, firmly controlled by the McGovern forces, voted 1,486 to 1,372 to unseat the delegates of Richard J. Daley. The people loyal to the man who routinely produced the largest Democratic majorities of any American big city were replaced by 59 reformers led by Jesse Jackson. For Chicago, it was a political earthquake. The party regulars had been booted from their own convention.

For the long-suffering foes of the Daley machine, though, it was a moment of the highest jubilation. On the convention floor that hot July evening, the new delegates rejoiced. Theodore H. White observed with wonder "the sight of black people jumping and hugging each other with glee as Dick Daley was humiliated."

Over the next four nights, through the platform debates, through the nomination and acceptance speech of George McGovern, the television cameras kept returning to the Illinois standard where, in the words of Gary Hart, McGovern's manager, there "loomed the imperious, almost regal countenance of the dashiki-clad Jesse Jackson. The saucer-shaped Martin Luther King medallion around his neck stood out like a beacon."

After the convention, McGovern's prospects sank like a stone. Running on a platform far to the left of the political mainstream, he managed to make the not particularly popular incumbent, Richard M. Nixon, unbeatable. In November, McGovern swept Massachusetts and the District of Columbia; Nixon carried the 49 remaining states.

Even so, 1972 was a political watershed for Chicago blacks. After the Democratic convention, Jackson had returned to the Illinois city and begun a campaign to defeat two Daley Democrats. One was Roman Pucinski, running for the U.S. Senate against Republican Charles Percy. The other, and for Jackson the far more important target, was Edward Hanrahan, the Cook County state's attorney (prosecutor).

In December 1969, Hanrahan had directed police officers to make an early-morning raid on a headquarters of the militant Black Panther party. The police, investigators later discovered, fired more than 100 shots, in the process killing 2 Panther leaders. Hanrahan and Daley declared the raid a triumph for

Jackson chats with George McGovern at a 1972 PUSH banquet in Chicago. The event, which drew 10,000 high-paying diners, raised much-needed funds for Jackson's new movement and also provided much-needed political exposure for candidate McGovern, Jackson's choice for president.

law and order. Jackson called it murder and said Hanrahan must be voted out of office even if it meant casting a ballot for his Republican opponent, Bernard Carey.

"We're going to see to it that every black person in Chicago gets instructions on how to vote a split ticket," Jackson announced. Getting Chicagoans to vote Republican was only slightly less difficult than getting the crowd at Wrigley Field to pull for the Mets against the Cubs, but Jackson was as good as his word. With Ralph Metcalfe, an anti-Daley congressman, working the back rooms, Jackson hit the street. "Don't worry, I repeat, about Democrat and Republican," he told the crowds. "You ain't neither one, you're black, and you're trapped. White folks been saying black folks ain't sophisticated enough to split tickets, well, they just ain't been speaking our language."

On election night, it was Jackson's language that was spoken. Normally, the black wards of Chicago voted 90 percent Democratic. About this precentage voted for McGovern and Metcalfe, running for reelection. Yet Pucinski, on the same ticket, lost the South Side to Percy. And in the race for state's attorney, Chicago blacks vented their fury by giving Bernard Carey, the Republican, an amazing 62 percent of their votes.

Hanrahan's defeat was a crowbar thrown into the gears of the Daley machine. Using his powers of investigation as the new state's attorney, Carey probed Chicago's government, uncovered corruption nearly everywhere he looked, and ultimately secured the indictments and convictions of several close Daley associates. If Jackson had not got blacks to vote a split ticket on election day 1972, none of it would have happened.

The Democratic machine wheezed along—Daley won reelection easily in 1975—but the desertion of

Frozen by astonishment, two aides to Chicago mayor Daley, John Touhy (left) and Clyde Choate, serve as launching pads for a joyful Jackson at the 1972 Democratic National Convention. Prompting both the agony and the ecstasy was the news that Jackson's delegate slate had just defeated Daley's by a vote of 1,486 to 1,372.

black voters cost it a good deal of horsepower. When, just before Christmas 1976, the 74-year-old mayor dropped dead of a massive heart attack, the fabled Chicago organization virtually died with him.

As for Jackson's part in the emergence of black political independence, Ralph Metcalfe acknowledged that he "played a major role." However, in the congressman's view, Jackson did not "have the people who are willing to go from door-to-door and do the precinct work. They may pack his Saturday meetings, but the people don't go out and ring doorbells." Jackson answered such critics by saying simply, "I'm a tree shaker, not a jelly maker."

And at times during the 1970s, it seemed as though he and PUSH were shaking every tree in the

Visiting a high school in Soweto, an all-black district of Johannesburg, South Africa, Jackson joins students in the black power salute. The PUSH leader, who was cheered at every stop he made, told South Africa's blacks that their stuggle for freedom had much in common with the struggle of American blacks.

forest. PUSH organized protest marches, trade fairs, and forums on everything from tax reform to voter registration. It sent Jackson to Africa for talks with the continent's leaders and to Washington for meetings with the president and testimony before congressional committees. It sponsored all-star basketball games, a Christian revival, and, in 1974, Hank Aaron Day in honor of the Atlanta Braves outfielder who smashed the all-time home run record set by Babe Ruth.

Until the mid-1970s, the most significant work of PUSH was similar to the work previously done by Operation Breadbasket: securing agreements, or, as they came to be called, covenants, with large corporations. "If [blacks] account for 20 percent of a firm's sales," Jackson explained, "then that firm must give us 20 percent of its advertising dollar, 20 percent of its banking business, and 20 percent of its jobs."

Companies often gave up without a fight. Fearful of lost trade and disruptions in business, executives accepted covenants before the first picketers appeared. By early 1975, PUSH had secured covenants with Schlitz and Miller beers, Avon Products, Quaker Oats, and General Foods.

On January 15, 1975, Jackson was in Washington, D.C., planning to lead a demonstration at the White House in favor of jobs for young, unemployed blacks. Striding to his place at the head of the march, he passed through the columns of young demonstrators recruited by PUSH. As he did so, his expression grew as cold as the blustery winter day. Many, if not most, of the demonstrators were in no condition to protest anything. They were drunk. They were high on drugs.

Appalled, Jackson abruptly canceled the march. Even if there were jobs, who would hire these individuals? "The door of opportunity is open for our people," he said angrily, "but they are too drunk, too unconscious to walk through the door." He vowed to do something about it.

Over the next year, Jackson turned the focus of PUSH away from economics and toward education by launching PUSH-Excel, a campaign designed to encourage young blacks to stay in school and study, to abandon drugs and alcohol, and to develop a sense of self-esteem. By promoting self-help and old-fashioned morality, PUSH-Excel proposed to combat the problems of illiteracy, drug abuse, and teenage pregnancy that afflicted the nation's inner cities.

Develop your willpower, Jackson told young blacks: "For if you get willpower, you'll get voting power and you'll get political power and you'll get economic power and you'll get social prestige. If you get willpower, you'll have a power that the boss can't fire. You'll have a power that jail cells can't lock up."

Introduced first in a number of Chicago high schools, PUSH-Excel spread rapidly. By 1979, 22 school districts had implemented variations of the program, which required the active participation of not only students but of teachers, parents, and administrators. The programs that got off to the fastest, most enthusiastic start were those kicked off by Jackson himself. Students responded to him and his chant of "I am Somebody!"

For many youngsters, Jackson's campaign marked the first time anyone had asked them to excel at anything other than shooting jump shots or applying makeup. To the girls in his audiences, he said, "You cannot spend more time in school on the cultivation of your bosom than your books. If you are to be the right kind of woman, you cannot have a fully developed bottom and a half developed brain." The boys heard equally blunt talk: "You're not a man because you can make a baby. They can make babies through artificial insemination. Imbeciles can make babies. You're only a man if you can raise a baby, protect a baby, and provide for a baby."

The message was black self-reliance. "Nobody will stop us from killing ourselves," he would insist. "Nobody will make us catch up. We will have to rely on ourselves to overcome history."

In December 1977, Dan Rather of CBS News interviewed Jackson for the popular Sunday evening television program "60 Minutes." Millions of viewers heard Jackson describe PUSH-Excel's efforts to save the country's black youth by mobilizing schools and communities.

One of the show's viewers was a man propped up with pillows in the bed of a hospital room in Minneapolis. He was Hubert H. Humphrey, U.S. senator from Minnesota, once vice-president, once the Democratic nominee for president, the most respected liberal politician of his generation. He was dying of cancer. The next day, Humphrey placed a call to Joseph Califano, the secretary of Health, Education, and Welfare in the new Democratic administration of President Jimmy Carter.

In a weak, rasping voice, Humphrey asked Califano if he had watched "60 Minutes" the night before. The secretary said yes. "Well, then you saw what I saw," said Humphrey. "I want you to talk to Jesse Jackson and help him. He's doing something for

Inspired by Jackson's pitch for PUSH-Excel, Chicago high school students hand him written assurances that they will study harder, refuse drugs, and avoid casual sex. Jackson pulled few punches when he talked to teenagers: To the boys, for example, he said, "You're not a man because you can make a baby. Imbeciles can make babies. You're only a man if you can raise a baby."

those kids. I've talked to him this morning and told him I'd talk to you. Now you get down to your office and help him. Will you do that for me?"

Califano immediately summoned Jackson to Washington. The secretary was perhaps taken aback to hear his visitor say that the PUSH-Excel program was not yet fully developed and that, right at the moment, it did not need federal funding. But Califano would not take no for an answer. He said that a developed program was not really necessary and that the government would assist in putting together a surefire proposal to get some money.

A month later, PUSH-Excel received a federal grant for $45,000. Five months later, $400,000 rolled in. It was just the beginning. Between 1976 and 1982, 3 federal agencies granted PUSH-Excel $5 million.

Unfortunately, PUSH-Excel never got fully developed. "The problem with Jackson's program," Califano admitted, "was his inability to sustain its momentum when he was not present, its dependence on his charisma." A one-time PUSH enthusiast described what happened at Washington High

School in Los Angeles: "As long as Jackson was on hand, the program worked. At Washington the success rate in signing up students to commit to the program was excellent. The school administrators got behind it and clamped down on troublemakers or kids involved in drugs and illegal activities. But without Jackson's charisma, the kids gradually lost enthusiasm."

In school after school, the story was the same: PUSH-Excel offered no day-to-day provision to monitor student performance or to keep parents and teachers involved. "PUSH didn't push, except Jesse," concluded a New York youth director.

Worse, no one seemed to know how all the money was spent. "While Jesse was flying around the country, things in Chicago were in absolute chaos," said a PUSH official. When the federal government got around to auditing PUSH-Excel's books, it uncovered an accountant's nightmare. "Our problem is that the man keeping the records died, and the records don't seem to exist," said a government spokesman. Eventually, federal officials demanded repayment of an unaccounted-for $1.4 million. In 1988, PUSH-Excel agreed to repay $550,000 and the case was closed.

The days of cabinet secretaries anxious to fund such programs as PUSH-Excel ended with Ronald Reagan's election to the presidency in 1980. Convinced that the conservative Reagan administration was out to "discredit and destroy PUSH," Jackson returned to his earlier theme of black economic empowerment. In 1981, PUSH initiated a new campaign of boycotts against such companies as Coca-Cola, Burger King, and the Heublein Corporation, owner of Kentucky Fried Chicken.

The first boycott targets gave up in a hurry. In 1981, Coca-Cola agreed to increase its black-owned franchises and to place a black director on its board.

A year later, Heublein greatly expanded the number of Kentucky Fried Chicken franchises available to blacks, even agreeing to help finance some of the new owners. As for locating those blacks wishing to become owners and franchisees, the covenants included a special clause: "Operation PUSH has volunteered to help . . . identify qualified applicants." Jackson explained, "All we ever did was recommend a list."

The name Noah Robinson, Jr., appeared on more than one of the lists. In 1975, after nearly five years of not speaking to one another, Jackson telephoned Robinson and suggested they let the wound heal. "I'm preaching brotherhood, but I'm not practicing it," Jackson said. They made their peace. Each knew the other so well, and they knew, too, why they had such trouble getting along. "I'm not interested in making money. . . . It's hard for Noah to relate to my value system and its hard for me to relate to his," Jackson said. Robinson quickly took full advantage of the famous Jackson name. One month after Jackson signed the covenant with Coca-Cola, Robinson received a Coke distributorship. Just as Jackson began negotiating with Heublein, Robinson won a supplier contract with Kentucky Fried Chicken. When Jackson took on the fast-food chains, Robinson wound up with a string of Wendy's, Bojangles, and Church's Fried Chicken outlets in Chicago and New York.

"I'm not in business with him, never have been," Jackson insisted, and Robinson would forever wonder why not. He told friends he simply could not understand his half brother's lack of interest in getting rich. He understood ambition though, and, in late 1983, he had no trouble getting the point when Jackson revealed his newest idea: "I think I'm going to run for president of the United States." ◈

7

"OUR TIME HAS COME"

O N AUGUST 27, 1983, at the Lincoln Memorial in Washington, D.C., Jesse Jackson stood exactly where, precisely 20 years earlier, Martin Luther King, Jr., had delivered his most famous speech. "I have a dream," King had said to the tens of thousands who came to the nation's capital to march for civil rights, "that my four little children will one day live in a nation where they will not be judged by the color of their skin, but by the content of their character."

"We must continue to dream, but the dream of 1963 must be expanded to meet the realities of these times," said Jackson to the crowd observing the 20th anniversary of the March on Washington. It was time for blacks to assert their political power, for them to register and vote: "Hands that picked cotton in 1864 will pick a president in 1984," said Jackson.

President Ronald Reagan had to go, Jackson thundered, and African Americans, like David facing Goliath, could lay low "the repressive Reagan regime" with their votes. It was also time for blacks to run for office: "Run! Run from disgrace to amazing grace. Run! Run from the outhouse to the statehouse to the courthouse to the White House. Run! But hold on to your dreams."

Jackson surveys the crowd at Operation PUSH's annual voter-registration rally in Cleveland, Ohio. Year after year, Jackson had waged a nonstop campaign to persuade young blacks to register and vote. By 1983, thousands were willing and eager to cast their ballots—for Jackson himself.

Harold Washington, surprise successor to the mighty Dick Daley, confers with staunch supporter Jackson. Washington's capture of the Chicago mayoralty delighted the nation's blacks—especially, perhaps, the celebrated figure to whom Daley had once offered a job as a minor city functionary.

The crowd's cadence started during Jackson's speech and reached a crescendo as he finished. "Run, Jesse, run!" the audience at the Lincoln Memorial chanted over and over, louder and louder. "Run, Jesse, run!"

It was a cry Jackson had heard all through the spring and summer as he waged a voter-registration drive in the churches and schools of black America. Signing up at each Jackson stop, new voters made it plain for whom they wished to vote: "Run, Jesse, run." With broad hints that, yes, indeed, he might just run for president, Jackson did nothing to discourage their hopes.

A black president? Ever since the 1983 race for mayor of Chicago, anything seemed possible. In February, Harold Washington, a relatively obscure black congressman from Chicago's South Side, had won the Democratic mayoral nomination by beating two white candidates: Jane Byrne, the incumbent, and Richard M. Daley, son of the late boss. Two months later, in a bitter, racially polarized general election, Washington edged his Republican opponent, Bernard Epton, a white man whose theme song was "Bye, Bye Blackbird."

However narrow, Washington's victory sent an emotional charge through black communities everywhere. A number of big cities had elected black mayors, but Chicago, where Richard J. Daley once ruled and where Martin Luther King, Jr., had so visibly failed, was a city with very special symbolism. Jackson was as exhilarated as anyone over Washington's election.

Jackson was still infuriated, however, by the behavior of the party's leading liberals during the mayoral primary. Senator Edward M. Kennedy of Massachusetts had endorsed Byrne, and former vice-president Walter Mondale, the odds-on favorite for the 1984 presidential nomination, had backed Daley.

The siding of Kennedy and Mondale with the white candidates "forced us to consider new options," Jackson said. "One option, of course, was to take it. Another option was to withdraw. Another option came to me: Why don't we run somebody in the [presidential] primary?" That somebody, naturally, was Jesse Jackson.

The idea of a black running for president, however, was rooted in more than the ambition of one man. With remarkable uniformity, blacks believed Ronald Reagan hostile to their interests, and for three years, their anger at his administration had been rising steadily. Reagan's apparent indifference to civil rights, along with his policies of tax cuts for the wealthy, accelerated defense spending, and reduced social programs, seemed to them dangerously wrongheaded. Their dismay with the president placed them against the prevailing political wind; as the 1984 election approached, Reagan's popularity among whites was soaring, but blacks felt an increasing sense of political isolation.

Although the nation's black political leadership was opposed to Reagan, it was divided on the question of a Jackson candidacy, or, for that matter, of any black candidacy. An impressive number of black mayors and congressmen had already committed to Walter Mondale. The former vice-president, a protégé of Hubert Humphrey's, possessed a flawless record in support of civil rights and promised, if elected, to reverse the Reagan policies. Furthermore, Mondale had a chance to win; Jackson did not.

Joe Reed, a leading black Democrat from Alabama, summed up the feelings of many: "We elected to tell the truth, and that was, we didn't think Jesse could get nominated, and if he got the nomination, he couldn't win." Mayor Coleman Young of Detroit was more blunt: "Jesse has no experience and he has no platform and he has no chance." Virtually every black big-city mayor seemed to agree. Only Richard Hatcher of Gary, Indiana; Marion Barry of Washington, D.C.; and Kenneth Gibson of Newark, New Jersey, wound up in the Jackson camp.

By the fall of 1983, having heard the cry "Run, Jesse, run" from every audience he addressed, Jackson decided the "black leadership family" was very much out of touch with the black rank and file. On October 30, 1983, in an interview with Mike Wallace on CBS's "60 Minutes," he declared his candidacy. Four days later, he kicked off his campaign for the nomination with a 3½ hour rally at the Washington, D.C., Convention Center. "Our time has come," he announced.

Few presidential campaigns run with clocklike precision, and Jackson's, in its early days, was no exception. It was chaos, and Jackson admitted it: "No fund-raising machinery, no budget, no knowledge of how to rent a plane or how to deal with the Secret Service and the traveling press corps. We learned all that on the job."

The other candidates for the nomination— Mondale, Senators John Glenn of Ohio, Gary Hart of Colorado, Ernest Hollings of South Carolina, and Alan Cranston of California, former Florida governor Reubin Askew, and, in a last hurrah, George McGovern—all had far more impressive operations, bigger campaign bank accounts, and seasoned professionals running things. However, to no one's knowledge had a Glenn speech ever been interrupted by shouts of "Run, John, run," nor was Mike Wallace in the habit of offering Hart or Hollings 20 minutes of air time on the country's top-rated news program.

Mondale, always freshly barbered and wearing a dark suit, white shirt, and red tie, was miles in front. But although he had grabbed every endorsement in sight, when he started to speak in his nasal monotone, his listeners had to be forgiven for recalling the last time they had consulted an undertaker.

Jackson, by comparison, was a live wire. Gone were the leather jackets and dashikis—he now favored suits as conservative as Mondale's—but the electricity that had energized the old Saturday morning Breadbasket and PUSH convocations was still running at full current. Enormously proud that one of their own was in the race for the top prize, blacks responded to his oratory with a fervor the other candidates could only dream about. The white media, endlessly curious about black America's favorite son, lavished on him the interviews, magazine covers, and evening news soundbites that placed him in the stratosphere of celebrity.

At Christmastime, 1983, Jackson completely stole the political show by halting his campaign and flying to the Middle East, where he negotiated the release of Lieutenant Robert Goodman, a U.S. naval aviator being held prisoner by Syria. On December 4, 1983, while attacking a Syrian position in Lebanon, Goodman, a 27-year-old black bombardier-navigator, had been shot down and captured. (In one of its periodic military adventures in the Middle East, the United States had intervened to support the beleaguered government of Lebanon.) The Reagan administration seemed neither particularly concerned about Goodman's plight nor on good enough terms with Syria to negotiate his release.

Jackson, on the other hand, got on well with Syrian president Hafez al-Assad and with most other Arab heads of state. This amiability stretched back to 1979, when Jackson had toured the Middle East with a delegation of prominent American blacks. What prompted their visit was President Jimmy Carter's firing of Andrew Young, Jackson's old SCLC colleague, from his post as U.S. ambassador to the United Nations. Carter had dumped Young after learning of the ambassador's secret meeting with a representative from the Palestinian Liberation Organization (PLO), the militant group demanding the

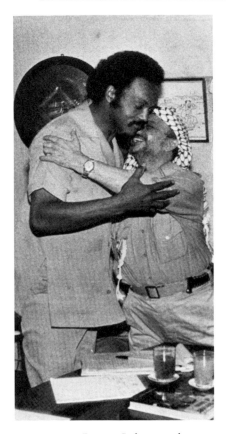

Visiting Beirut, Lebanon, during his 1979 tour of the Mideast, Jackson gets a hug from Yasir Arafat, leader of the Palestine Liberation Organization.
Jackson's cordial relationship with Arafat infuriated many supporters of Israel, but it paved the way for the American politician's future negotiations with the Arab world.

establishment of an independent Palestinian state on territory occupied by Israel.

Black leaders hit the ceiling at Young's dismissal. Some accused American Jews of pressuring Carter; others denounced the traditional American policy of unswerving support for Israel. On tour in the Middle East, Jackson was photographed embracing PLO leader Yasir Arafat and leading a number of largely puzzled Palestinians in the "I am Somebody" chant. His conduct appalled Israelis and American Jews, just as surely as it delighted the Arab world.

So it was that when Jackson appealed to Syria for the release of Lieutenant Goodman, President Assad replied with an invitation to come and talk things over. Trailed by a retinue of clergymen, aides, Secret Service agents, and reporters, Jackson headed for Damascus. It was risky business. He had received no official encouragement at all—Reagan refused his telephone call—and a skeptical press was calling the trip shameless grandstanding. Even the airman's father, fearful that intervention might worsen his son's plight, asked Jackson not to go.

In Damascus, Jackson argued with Syrian officials that freeing Goodman would break the "circle of pain" in American-Syrian relations. After one lengthy conference, he suggested concluding with a prayer and turned to a fellow American, Nation of Islam leader Louis Farrakhan, who delivered an Islamic prayer in faultless Arabic. This display both touched and impressed the Syrians. Three days later, on January 3, 1984, Syrian officials summoned Jackson and handed him good news: Goodman was a free man.

JESSE DID IT! screamed the headline of the *New York Daily News*. Even Jackson's political rivals had to hand it to him. "It is impressive, yes," said Walter Mondale. As soon as their plane touched down in Washington, Jackson and Goodman sped to the

White House for a ceremonial welcome home by President Reagan.

In the Rose Garden, with Vice-president George Bush and cabinet members forming a solemn tableau, Jackson was the radiant star. "Reverend Jackson's mission was a personal mission of mercy and he has earned our gratitude and admiration," the president said. His tone was gracious, but he was far from pleased by Assad's turning Goodman over to a political foe.

In one bold stroke, Jackson had dramatically answered the noisy critics who said he was all talk. New life surged through his campaign for president. A poll of Democrats in New Hampshire, site of the first primary and a state with a tiny black population, put him in third place with 16 percent of the vote.

Then, with one stroke more, he threw away nearly all he had won.

On the morning of January 25, 1984, Jackson arrived at Washington's National Airport and, before his plane took off, dropped into the cafeteria for breakfast. When he saw Milton Coleman, a black *Washington Post* reporter covering his campaign, he waved him over to his table. "Let's talk black," Jackson said. It was something he frequently said to black correspondents—his way of declaring that the conversation that followed would be off the record. Coleman understood that in any story he wrote, nothing Jackson said could be directly attributed to him.

The talk turned to an upcoming meeting at which Jackson and several *Washington Post* editors would discuss the candidate's views on foreign policy. Questions about Israel, Coleman said, were certain to be asked. Fine, said Jackson, but he would not be intimidated. He continued: "All hymie wants to talk about is Israel. Everytime you go to hymietown, that's all they want to talk about."

Lieutenant Robert Goodman, an American naval flier shot down and captured by Syria in late 1983, matches the broad smile flashed by his rescuer. Ignoring skepticism from the Ronald Reagan administration and the American public, Jackson had flown to Damascus and persuaded the Syrians to release Goodman.

"Hymie" was new to Coleman, but he assumed, correctly, that Jackson was referring to Jews and that "hymietown" meant New York, the city with the nation's largest Jewish population. For the time being, Coleman did nothing. "I filed it away in my head," he recalled.

But when he learned that other black reporters had heard Jackson say much the same thing, Coleman decided to pass the information along to Rick Atkinson, a *Post* reporter who was writing a story about Jackson's chilly relations with Jews. On Monday, February 13, Atkinson's story appeared in the *Post*. Near the end were two brief paragraphs:

> In private conversations with reporters, Jackson has referred to Jews as "hymie" and to New York as "hymietown."
>
> "I'm not familiar with that," Jackson said Thursday. "That's not accurate."

The revelation soon became front-page news. On February 18, the *Post* editorialized that Jackson's hymie remarks were "ugly," "degrading," and "disgusting." Jackson, said the paper, should present "an explanation and an apology." Five days later, the *New York Times* finally offered its first coverage of the incident. By then, leaders of Jewish organizations were expressing outrage at Jackson's slur.

For the best part of two weeks, Jackson stuck to his denial. On "Face the Nation," he said, "It simply isn't true, and I think the accuser ought to come forth." That satisfied no one in the press, and the controversy gathered fury.

On February 25, the storm nearly became a hurricane. It was Savior's Day, a holy event on the calendar of the Nation of Islam, the Black Muslim sect led by Louis Farrakhan. A mesmerizing speaker, Farrakhan was a regular at Jackson rallies, warming up the crowd, then introducing the candidate, which was what he did on Savior's Day in Chicago.

With Jackson a few feet away, Farrakhan declared: "I say to the Jewish people who may not like our brother, when you attack him you attack the millions who are lining up with him. You are attacking all of us. If you harm this brother, I warn you in the name of Allah, this will be the last one you do harm." Jackson listened and, in his own speech, said nothing to contradict Farrakhan's open threat to the nation's Jews.

Jackson's advisers were horrified: Matters were bad enough without this apparent tolerance for Farrakhan. Now, said several Jackson staffers, unless something was done right away, the entire campaign might explode. The day after his appearance with Farrakhan, Jackson went before a candidates' forum at a crowded synagogue in Manchester, New Hampshire. "In private talks we sometimes let our guard down and we become thoughtless," he said. "It was not in a spirit of meanness, an off-color remark having no bearing on politics. . . . However innocent or unintended, it was wrong."

But damage had been done. On February 28, Jackson captured only five percent of the primary vote in New Hampshire, finishing a poor fourth behind Hart, Mondale, and Glenn. What was worse,

Forced to honor Jackson because of his rescue of Goodman, Ronald Reagan acts the genial host in the White House Oval Office. The president said Jackson had earned the nation's "gratitude and admiration," but insiders knew he was seething about the Democratic contender's coup.

Farrakhan continued to breathe fire into the controversy. In a March 11 radio broadcast, the minister announced that Milton Coleman, the black reporter who had revealed Jackson's hymie remark, was a "traitor," a "Judas," and an "Uncle Tom." Farrakhan issued a warning to Coleman: "One day we will punish you with death." The Nation of Islam leader also found something nice to say about the German dictator Adolf Hitler: "The Jews don't like Farrakhan, so they call me Hitler. Well, that's a good name. Hitler was a very great man."

Editorialists outdid one another in expressing outrage at Farrakhan's threatening message to Coleman and his praise of Hitler. Even Jackson's rivals for the Democratic nomination, who up until then had kept quiet, roused themselves. Mondale called Farrakhan's remarks "an outrage," and Hart said that if he were Jackson, he "would repudiate the support of Mr. Farrakhan."

Jackson did not particularly care what Gary Hart thought he should do. In February, Jackson had publicly apologized at the New Hampshire synagogue, and he was not about to make it a monthly habit. He severed whatever remaining ties Farrakhan had to the campaign, said his threat to Coleman was "wrong," and condemned the minister's "message." But he refused to condemn the messenger. "Jesus repudiated the politics of assassination," said Jackson, "but he did not repudiate Judas." His mind was set. Despite badgering from the press and pleas from prominent Democrats, Jackson would not repudiate Farrakhan.

"I felt very black at this point," Jackie Jackson recalled. "White people were saying now, little children, you're not grown up. . . . I thought it was very arrogant of white people to ask us to explain Farrakhan, to ask us to disassociate ourselves from him. . . . We were treated very colored."

Nation of Islam leader and longtime Jackson supporter Louis Farrakhan addresses a Boston audience in the mid-1980s. His unconcealed anti-Semitism made him a huge political liability for presidential hopeful Jackson, who denounced only Farrakhan's message, not the man himself.

A great many blacks agreed. Beginning in February with the hymie story and on into the spring with the Farrakhan storm, Jackson's support among blacks grew both broader and deeper. His hopes of winning anything beyond a token vote from whites evaporated with the controversy, but black ballots would sustain him through the primaries.

"We are the poorest campaign, with the richest message," said Jackson at nearly every stop as he flew from state to state in a slow, creaking Lockheed Electra, a relic from the prejet age. After New Hampshire, the scene shifted to the South, where, on March 13, Super Tuesday, Alabama, Georgia, and Florida voted. Jackson still lacked money and organization, but he was back home, and that was sufficient for many black voters in the Deep South. His campaign tapped the wellspring of black pride. "He makes me feel sooo good," exulted a young black student. A black schoolteacher said it did not matter whether Jackson won or not. Pointing to her class, she said, "Just so they have somebody to look up to. Just so we have somebody to idolize." "He's us, that's all," said a black nurse.

With its large black population, the South could have been friendly territory for Jackson on Super Tuesday. But Mondale, with the support of the region's black leadership, cut into his strength. In Alabama, Birmingham mayor Richard Arrington put his political organization to work for the former vice-president. In Georgia, Coretta Scott King and Andrew Young, now mayor of Atlanta, also did what they could for Mondale. On primary day, Jackson captured roughly 20 percent of the vote in Alabama and Georgia and 12 percent in Florida.

After Super Tuesday, the race for the Democratic nomination came down to three men: Mondale, Hart, and Jackson. Mondale, weighted down by all his endorsements, had stumbled badly coming out of the blocks, losing New Hampshire to the youthful-looking Hart. But by winning Alabama, Georgia, and, a week later, Illinois, he reestablished himself as the front-runner. In April, he flattened Hart in the New York and Pennsylvania primaries, virtually assuring himself of the nomination.

Jackson placed third in each of the northern primaries, sweeping the big-city black vote. Black politicians stood by Mondale, but it was getting very lonely for them. In Pennsylvania, Mayor Wilson Goode of Philadelphia boosted Mondale; 78 percent of the city's black voters supported Jackson. Representative Charles Rangel of New York also recommended Mondale; 87 percent of black New Yorkers cast ballots for Jackson.

"I want to be respected and heard," Jackson said, and he attained those goals, thanks largely to a series of televised debates. "Jackson had the greatest natural ease and assurance of any Democratic candidate," wrote William A. Henry III of the candidates' encounter at Columbia University during the New York campaign. "He had an almost intuitive gift for making exactly the right adjustments of manner and intonation to fit any circumstance."

Jackson realized that a lot was riding on each appearance. "Suppose I had made big classical errors in the debates," he later said to columnists Jules Witcover and Jack Germond. "It would have embarrassed my people. They would have said, 'You know, I told you we were not ready.'"

They said anything but. "I see Jesse on TV with all those big people, and I just puff up. I know he's not going to be president, but he could be," said a black Philadelphian.

While Jackson more than held his own in the televised debates, he steadily lost ground in the process of selecting delegates to the Democratic convention. The system favored a candidate such as Mondale, one who had the backing of party bigwigs and showed strength among all groups of Democrats. It worked against Jackson, whose great strength was among blacks. (In Pennsylvania, for example, he got only three percent of the white vote.) After all the primaries had been run and all the delegates had been named, Jackson had 21 percent of the popular vote, but only 11 percent of the delegates.

In June, following the final primaries, Jackson took off on a swing through Central America and Cuba. Presidential candidates traditionally campaigned within the borders of the United States, but Jackson was hardly a traditional candidate. His journey to Panama, El Salvador, Cuba, and Nicaragua dramatized his strong opposition to the U.S. government's policies in the region. Since it had seized power in 1959, Fidel Castro's Communist regime in Cuba had endured the near total enmity of every American president, Democrat and Republican alike. The Reagan administration, which had worked up a similar hatred of Nicaragua's Sandinista government, openly sponsored an anti-Sandinista military insurgency, the Contras.

Jackson, in common with the American left, believed "we must completely reverse Ronald Rea-

Taking time out after a grueling season of primaries in 1984, the 42-year-old Jackson prepares to shoot a few baskets in the backyard of his Chicago home.

Cuban leader Fidel Castro greets Jackson at Havana's Presidential Palace in June 1984. Repeating his Syrian success of early in the year, Jackson persuaded Castro to let him take almost 50 prisoners—22 of them Americans—back to the United States. This time, Americans had mixed reactions: Some applauded; others accused Jackson of overstepping his role as a private citizen.

gan's policies in Central America." He favored assisting the Sandinistas "in their attempt to build a more just society" and advocated normal diplomatic relations with Cuba. "We have much to learn from the Cubans," he insisted. "They have much to learn from us."

Castro gave the "Moral Offensive"—Jackson's name for his journey—its warmest reception. Meeting the American's plane at the Havana airport, the Cuban leader said, "He honors us with his visit."

Jackson reciprocated. The next afternoon, speaking at the University of Havana, he proclaimed: "Long live Cuba! Long live the United States! Long live Castro! Long live Martin Luther King! Long live Che Guevara! Long live our cry of freedom! Our time has come." It was not every day a candidate for the Democratic presidential nomination linked the name of America's great apostle of nonviolence with those of Castro and his aide Guevara.

Later the same day, Jackson led Castro into the First Methodist Church of Havana and offered a prayer for peace. "I'll fear no evil, for Thou art with me," he prayed. "Thy rod and Thy staff comfort me." Then he added, "Hold on, Cuba! Hold on, Castro! Hold on, Nicaragua!"

Jackson did not leave Cuba empty-handed. Castro agreed to release into Jackson's custody 22 Americans and 26 Cubans being held in Cuba's prisons. Most of the Americans had been convicted of drug dealing and smuggling. The Cubans had been imprisoned for what the Castro government labeled "behavior injurious to the nation"—in short, political dissent.

Jackson brought nearly 50 newly released prisoners home with him, but this rescue, unlike that of Lieutenant Goodman, produced only muted acclaim. While some Americans applauded Jackson's Cuban mission, others wondered about the propriety of a private citizen dealing with the head of a Communist state. Speaking for many of Jackson's critics, James Reston of the *New York Times* said flatly, "He is interfering with the constitutional rights of the president and Congress to conduct foreign policy."

The controversy whipped up by Jackson's Central American excursion did not last very long. Within two weeks of his return, the Democratic National Convention opened in San Francisco. ❧

8

"WE'RE WINNING"

❧

ONE EVENING IN late 1983, after a long campaign day, Walter Mondale was having a drink with reporters in the bar of a New Hampshire motel. "How are you going to handle Jesse?" he was asked.

Mondale puffed his cigar, then replied with a laugh, "Veerry carefully."

Throughout the campaign, Mondale did exactly that. While he slugged away at Gary Hart and the others, with Jackson he pulled his punches or did not even swing. "What I decided to do," Mondale later explained to Jack Germond and Jules Witcover, "was to disagree in a dignified way with Jesse Jackson . . . and try to give him the dignity and respect he deserved as a candidate for president, to recognize the profound nature of this new effort by a black in America and what it meant to millions of black Americans." The former vice-president feared that anything beyond the gentlest criticism of Jackson would alienate millions of blacks whose votes Mondale required if he was to stand a chance of defeating Ronald Reagan. In other words, he had to have Jackson's goodwill and endorsement.

About to deliver his eagerly awaited 1984 convention speech in San Francisco, Jackson offers his admirers a buoyant salute. He went on to stun them with the campaign's most electrifying oratory: "Leave the racial battleground" for the "moral high ground," he urged. "America, our time has come!"

He was not to win them easily. Jackson knew that as long as he withheld an endorsement, he would remain at the center of things, the subject of speculation and attention—a major player in the Democratic party. He tried to make the most of his position, pressing demands on Mondale and hinting he might sit out the fall campaign. As they gathered in San Francisco for their convention in July, nearly every Democrat seemed to be asking, What does Jesse want?

For one thing, he wanted changes in the platform, calling on the party to endorse stronger measures for affirmative action, a reduction in defense spending, a policy of no first use of nuclear weapons, and an end to the system of runoff primaries when no candidate got a majority—a system, Jackson argued, that discriminated against blacks. Already under attack for being too liberal, Mondale had no wish to let the platform drift further to the left and rejected each Jackson proposal.

The sole concession Mondale made to Jackson was handing him a prime-time spot for his speech to the convention—eight o'clock eastern time, Tuesday evening. Neither Mondale nor anyone else knew what Jackson planned to say. Robert Beckel, who had negotiated with Jackson on Mondale's behalf and who had given him the 8:00 P.M. slot, tried to get a preview of Jackson's text. "You've really got to give a great speech," he said as he and Jackson stood on a balcony of the Fairmont Hotel and gazed at the San Francisco skyline. "I've got a lot invested in you."

"Well, I'll tell you this, Beckel," replied Jackson, delighting in the nervousness of the Mondale camp. "You're either going to be a chimp, a chump, or a champ."

As the time for Jackson's speech approached, Dan Rather on CBS was promising great things. This speech was going to be something; get the whole family together, the anchorman advised, even "get grandma in." By now, much of the country wanted to know, What does Jesse want? His speech drew the largest television audience of the convention.

He began with what amounted to an apology for the hymietown remark and the Farrakhan mess. "If in my low moments, in word, deed, or attitude, through some error of temper, taste, or tone, I have caused any discomfort, created pain, or revived someone's fears, that was not my truest self," he said. "As I develop and serve, be patient. God is not finished with me yet."

Jackson was in top form. He spoke of his constituency as "the damned, the disinherited, the disrespected, and the despised," and of America as "a rainbow—red, yellow, brown, black, and white—we're all precious in God's sight." He laced into the policies of the Reagan administration and issued a call for Democratic unity: "We are much too intelligent, much too bound by our Judeo-Christian heritage, much too victimized by racism, sexism, militarism, and anti-Semitism, much too threatened as historical scapegoats to go on divided from one another." He concluded: "Our time has come! No lie can live forever. Our time has come. We must leave the racial battleground and come to the economic common ground and the moral high ground. America, our time has come!"

Jackson's address was the high point of the convention, perhaps of the 1984 Democratic campaign. When Mondale delivered his acceptance speech two nights later, he seized the moment to tell the nation he planned, if elected, to raise everybody's taxes. Mondale wound up in November carrying only the District of Columbia and his home state of Minnesota. Reagan, who had proclaimed that it was "morning again in America," won all the rest.

There was never the slightest doubt that Jackson meant to run for the 1988 nomination. With the ashes of the Mondale disaster still glowing, he announced the formation of the National Rainbow Coalition, a political action committee designed to publicize and finance his activities until the 1988 campaign officially began. He traveled the country incessantly, building grass-roots support, appealing to those who were having a hard time.

This time, Jackson planned a broader-based and more professional organization. "In 1984 we went through the experience of an exhilarating campaign, but we were all spirit and not much body," he explained to a supporter in early 1986. "We need both ministers, who were our original base, and politicians, but now we need politicians more so we're not labeled some kind of fringe. We've got to expand the Rainbow Coalition."

No one would label Gerald Austin "some kind of fringe." A well-regarded professional who had run several successful campaigns in Ohio, Austin signed on as Jackson's campaign manager. He was committed to the Jackson cause. "Before I took this job I traveled a few days . . . with Jackson to see how we got on," he told Elizabeth Colton, the campaign press secretary. "After I saw him in action a few times, I began to think: This guy can go all the way. Jesse Jackson can be elected president. And that's the way I'm now running this campaign."

On October 24, 1987, in Raleigh, North Carolina, Jackson formally announced his candidacy. "I want to be president of the United States of America," he said. His competition for the Democratic nomination was, if anything, less imposing than it had been in 1984. Back for a second go at it, Gary Hart had the look of a front-runner, but he careened into the starting post. In the spring of 1987, less than a week after announcing his candidacy, he was found to be keeping steady nighttime company with a woman decidedly not his wife. A few days later, after facing such questions from reporters as "Have you

After officially announcing his candidacy for the 1988 Democratic presidential nomination before a crowd in Raleigh, North Carolina, Jackson kisses his wife and gets set to battle for the prize. Pitted against five white candidates, he started fast, shooting to the front of the pack in the early stages of the race.

ever committed adultery?" Hart gave up and withdrew from the race.

The vacuum created by Hart's pullout was not easily filled. Although Democratic prospects looked brighter than they had four years earlier, the party stars—Governor Mario Cuomo of New York and Senator Sam Nunn of Georgia—left the stage to their understudies. In Cuomo's case, it was another northeastern governor, Michael Dukakis of Massachusetts, and in Nunn's, it was Senator Albert Gore, Jr., of Tennessee. Rounding out the field, hoping for

lightning to strike, were Representative Richard
Gephardt of Missouri, Senator Paul Simon of Illinois,
and former governor Bruce Babbitt of Arizona.

The good news for Jackson was that few voters
knew anything about these candidates. Everybody, of
course, had heard of Jackson; on the basis of name
recognition, he shot to the front of the public-
opinion polls. Furthermore, none of the white candidates had anything resembling Mondale's ties to
the black community. This time around, Jackson
could count on rock-solid black support.

He was dealt another ace with the revised sched-
ule of the nominating process. Eager to nominate a
moderate white southerner, conservative Democrats
had prevailed on party officials to group together 14
southern primaries on a single election day, Super
Tuesday, March 8, 1988. They hoped a moderate, by
sweeping the South, would pick up enough momentum to be unstoppable. They miscalculated badly. It
was Jackson, the exact opposite of a white moderate,
whose interests were served by the Super Tuesday
strategy. His best states, by virtue of their large black
populations, were in the South.

In the two weeks prior to Super Tuesday, Jackson
crisscrossed the South, rallying his loyal constituency
and reaching across the past to old foes. After a
speech in Beaumont, Texas, for example, he met
Bruce Hill, a local union leader. "Back in 1965 I was
with you in Selma," Hill said. Clearly delighted,
Jackson at once started talking about the great battle
against white supremacy. Hill interrupted: "No, no.
I was there, but I was on the other side." He had
been a member of the Ku Klux Klan. Jackson stared
at him. "But Jesse, today I'm on your side!" Hill
exclaimed.

The men embraced. "It summed up the beauty
and the promise of the Jackson campaign: He was the
candidate willing to reach out to anyone," journalist

Walter Fauntroy, Washington, D.C.'s nonvoting congressional representative, links arms with Jackson and Coretta Scott King during a demonstration in the nation's capital. King's belated but welcome 1988 acceptance of Jackson as her husband's heir supplied the Jackson campaign with a powerful shot in the arm.

Roger Simon wrote of the incident. "Even to those who had once despised him or had shouted racial epithets at him or had tried to lynch him."

There were other such moments. In Selma itself, Jackson was greeted by Joe T. Smitherman, then as in 1965 the town's mayor. Twenty-three years earlier, he too had been on the other side. Now, he gave Jackson the key to the city and then joined him for a walk across the infamous Edmund Pettus Bridge, site of Bloody Sunday. Smitherman admitted he had been wrong all those years before, and Jackson, deeply touched, said it was time "to forgive each other, redeem each other, and move on."

On Sunday afternoon, March 6, two days before the voting, Jackson attended worship services at the Ebenezer Baptist Church in Atlanta, the church of Martin Luther King, Jr. Visiting the historic church four years earlier, on the eve of 1984's Super Tuesday, Jackson had been pointedly snubbed by the King family, few of whom turned out to hear him preach.

On this Sunday, however, Coretta Scott King accompanied Jackson to her husband's tomb. Together they laid a wreath on the grave and together they prayed. These actions held great significance. However reluctantly, with whatever misgivings, Coretta King had symbolically passed the torch of leadership to Jesse Jackson.

On Super Tuesday, Jackson did well—very well. He won the primaries of 5 states (Georgia, Alabama, Louisiana, Mississippi, and Virginia), placed second in the remaining southern states, and captured 353 delegates to the national convention. Dukakis won in Texas and Florida, and in the five northern and western states voting that day. Gore of Tennessee salvaged a little of the original plan behind Super Tuesday by carrying five states in the upper South.

The race was left with three candidates: Jackson, Dukakis, and Gore. Dukakis offered himself as the cool, experienced master of public policy, the creator and guardian of the Massachusetts Miracle, his state's supposedly booming economy. Uncertain about which face to present to the electorate, Gore settled on promoting a hawkish foreign policy and deriding his opponents as advocates of "retreat, complacency, and despair."

Jackson plainly stood to the left of his two adversaries. While Gore and Dukakis accepted certain aspects of the Reagan years, such as lower tax rates and big defense budgets, Jackson demanded radical change. On the campaign trail, he directed his sharpest remarks at huge multinational corporations—"barracudas," he called them—that did "economic violence" by opening plants abroad.

"Your jobs went to South Korea and Taiwan and South Africa and Chile," Jackson told the unemployed. The government, he said, had to control private enterprise to the extent that "its investment decisions are made in the best interests of the community." Jackson envisioned a vastly expanded welfare state, offering comprehensive health care, new housing projects, bigger welfare checks, and larger food stamp benefits. To pay for it, he would cut defense spending, raise taxes, and borrow against public-employee pension funds.

After Super Tuesday, the primary trail led north, first to Illinois, where Jackson ran second to Simon— whose candidacy had been diminished to "favorite-son" status—and then to Michigan. Jackson did not go into Michigan with very high hopes. Dukakis had the backing of the Michigan party apparatus and an ally in Mayor Coleman Young of Detroit, one of the handful of black elected officials in the country not supporting Jackson.

Well before the Michigan voting, Dukakis stopped campaigning and returned to Boston to look after some state business. His private polls showed him 10 points ahead of Jackson (Gore was not contesting the state), and he figured he had it wrapped up. Coleman Young, however, was not so sure. On election eve, he attended a Greek-American fund-raiser with a Dukakis aide. Fifteen hundred people wildly cheered every mention of Dukakis, a fellow Greek American. "You see how excited these people are about Michael?" Young asked the aide. "I got a whole city like that for Jesse."

On Saturday evening, the Dukakis high command gathered at its Boston headquarters, ready to watch the vote from Michigan and celebrate the inevitable triumph. But early on, things started going very wrong. As the votes poured in, Dukakis's shocked media adviser asked, "Jesus, where are all these black people coming from?"

They came from the old factory towns of Flint and Lansing and from the housing projects and neighborhoods of Detroit. In overwhelming numbers, they gave up their Saturday for Jesse Jackson. In the 2 congressional districts of Detroit, 50,000 people voted. One district went 25–1 for Jackson, the other

Jackson and influential Democrat Clark Clifford emerge from a spring 1988 conference to talk to reporters about the new "bonding of the Democratic party." During the meeting, representatives of several candidates who had dropped from the race—and who had once savagely criticized Jackson—offered him their assistance.

17–1. By casting approximately 45 percent of the total vote, Michigan blacks handed Jackson a stunning victory. The final statewide count: Jackson, 55 percent; Dukakis, 29 percent.

On Monday evening, March 28, Dan Rather led off the "CBS Evening News" by announcing, "Jesse Jackson has become the front-runner." *Newsweek* devoted its lead to the "Michigan Miracle." *Time* splashed his photograph on its cover with the caption, "Jackson!?" In the accompanying story, the news magazine reported that "for the first time in the nation's history, a major political party was grappling with one of the biggest what-ifs of all: What if Democratic voters actually nominate a black man for president?"

The white elders of the party, who four years earlier had not given Jackson the time of day, started wondering the same thing, and a few tried to accommodate themselves to the changed political landscape. In early April, Jackson met a group of Democratic leaders over breakfast in a private dining room of the Jefferson Hotel in Washington. Clark Clifford, a courtly, white-haired, impeccably tailored Washington lawyer whose days of influence stretched back to the Truman administration of the late 1940s, assured the candidate that there was no "Stop Jackson" movement. If Jackson happened to be nominated, said Clifford, he would have the benefit of "the best brains the party and the country have to offer."

Despite Clifford's encouraging words, not a single senator, governor, or state chairman endorsed Jackson. In the Wisconsin primary of April 5, he captured only 28 percent of the vote; Dukakis won with 48 percent and was quickly reestablished as the likely nominee. Michigan, the pundits now said, had been a fluke.

Jackson had a chance to prove them wrong. On April 19, New York voted, and on the face of it, his prospects looked good. More than a quarter of the votes in New York were cast by blacks, and this time, Gore was making a stand. In a 3-man race, with 40 or 45 percent of the vote, Jackson might win.

In New York, however, Jews also accounted for a quarter of the electorate; for them, Jackson's hymie-town remark and his association with Farrakhan were vivid memories. And if by chance people had forgotten, Edward I. Koch, mayor of New York, was around to help them remember.

"I'm the Paul Revere," said the mayor as he galloped off to warn voters about Jackson. In fact, he was the head of a city whose racial relations were as poisonous as any in the country. Energetic and colorful, Koch had enjoyed wide popularity during his first two terms, but his abrasive style—"slime," "dummy," "poverty pimp," and "wacko" were favored descriptions of his political rivals—had also fueled the fire between black and white.

After endorsing Gore, Koch dragged the Tennessee senator around the city to the usual campaign stops but paid him scant attention. It was Jackson he was after. "And he thinks maybe Jews and other supporters of Israel should vote for him?" Koch said of Jackson. "They have got to be crazy!" Then came

In August 1988, four months after New York's bitter and divisive primary, Jackson offers a handshake of truce to New York City mayor Ed Koch. Standing between the two is Manhattan Borough President David Dinkins, who was to become, in 1989, the city's first black mayor.

the Koch litany: Jackson was against Israel; he would, if elected president, "bankrupt the country in three weeks and leave it defenseless in six weeks."

"Ed Koch is an idiot, even by New York standards," replied Gerald Austin. Jackson was unhappy with the remark. "You keep forgetting," he informed Austin, "you're the campaign manager, I'm the spokesman." Jackson preferred not to get into the gutter with Koch.

He also preferred not to try to improve relations with New York's Jews, avoiding Jewish groups and refusing to march in the big Salute to Israel Parade on Fifth Avenue just before election day. Jews, he was certain, had their mind made up about him: "Children in this city have been taught to fear. That's not right. Jewish children have been taught to fear me. That's not right."

"Jesse showed contempt and arrogance!" Koch bellowed after Jackson failed to show up for the parade. "He is treating Jews with contempt and arrogance."

There were times when Jackson wanted to let the mayor have it, but he continued his discreet, turn-the-other-cheek approach. "In some sense I came out of New York victorious, because my mettle under heat was shown," he reflected later. "I had the capacity to take a punch without my knees buckling. And enough strength not to react, to keep my composure."

He did not come out of New York victorious in any conventional sense. Dukakis won the primary with 51 percent of the vote. Jackson polled 37 percent, and Gore, smothered by the mayor's embrace, trailed with 10 percent.

The bright optimism that had followed the Michigan Miracle was gone for good. For three wonderful weeks, it had been castles in the air for Jackson and his entourage as they considered vice-presidential

Jackson demonstrates his campaign skills at an Iowa farm. Like any sensible politician, he knew that winning voters' hearts involves more than defining issues and taking positions: Equally crucial are cow milking, baby kissing, and hand shaking.

candidates, cabinet appointments, and new directions in foreign policy. Now, with New York's vote counted, Jackson stood before his cheering supporters in the Sheraton Centre. His eyes glistened with tears. Beside him, Jackie was weeping.

"Dr. Martin Luther King's heart is rejoicing tonight," he said. "We're winning. We've climbed the tough side of the mountain and we can keep on climbing, step by step by step."

In 1988, there were not many more steps for him to take. After New York, Gore sensibly withdrew, reducing the field to Dukakis and Jackson. It was one on one, black against white, a race Jackson could not win. Over the next six weeks, Dukakis pounded Jackson in primaries from Pennsylvania to California. And, as Mondale had done four years before, the governor handled Jackson with kid gloves, ignoring his program and campaign but refusing to criticize him.

After Dukakis won the party's nomination that July, Jackson dutifully campaigned for him, traveling the country in a chartered jet and urging his audiences to register and to vote Democratic. Dukakis

left most blacks cold, but on election day, 9 out of 10 voted for him—a showing for which Jackson could rightfully claim much of the credit. But in spite of Jackson's effective electioneering, Dukakis fell flat on his face. After running a dull, confused campaign, he saw George Bush cruise to an easy victory in November.

In early 1989, as Bush was settling into the White House, Jackson announced that he was moving from Chicago to Washington, D.C. The change of address sparked instant rumors that Jackson intended to run for mayor of the District of Columbia, a city whose vast, poor, overwhelmingly black sections were wracked by crime and virtually ruled by drug dealers. If he decided to run for mayor, he would, given his great popularity in the District, almost certainly win.

And if Jackson became mayor of Washington, as Hendrick Hertzberg of the *New Republic* put it, "No longer could it be said that Jesse Jackson had never been elected anything, had never held public office." Jackson, however, had no interest in the job. "I want to serve," he said in March 1990, "but not as mayor." Instead, he announced himself as a candidate for statehood, or "shadow," senator from the District of Columbia, a new post created by the city government to lobby Congress for statehood. "Statehood for the District of Columbia," said Jackson, "is the most important civil rights and social justice issue in America today."

Facing minimal opposition and solidly supported by most Washingtonians, Jackson was confident about the election. At this point, however, his support among members of the black political establishment was far from solid. Black politicians knew they had to win the votes and confidence of whites to get elected. A number of these political figures—including Virginia's Douglas Wilder, the nation's first black governor; and David Dinkins, New York City's first black mayor—indicated that they considered

Jackson too controversial, too black. "The move is mainstream now," said a Dinkins associate.

Jackson's convention manager in Atlanta, Ron Brown, who in 1989 had become the first black to head the Democratic National Committee, echoed the sentiments of the Dinkins camp. Talking to a reporter about Jackson, Brown said, "Here is a guy who is brilliant, got great political instincts, been right on most of the issues . . . but as happens so often, not only in politics but in life, he just might not be the right message carrier."

The "right carrier" or not, Jackson swept to victory in the 1990 race for District of Columbia shadow senator. His new office paid no salary, had no budget, carried no clear responsibilities, and entitled its holder to no vote in Congress. Nevertheless, Jackson expected the Democrats in the Senate to admit him to their caucus and include him in their decision-making processes. "After traveling this country in two presidential campaigns and getting seven million votes," he declared, "I have *earned* the right to be part of the national governing body."

Three months before the election, in August 1990, Jackson heard the news that Iraq had invaded its neighbor, the oil-rich nation of Kuwait. Bush quickly responded by dispatching American troops to the Arabian desert, organizing international sanctions, and threatening Iraq's dictator, Saddam Hussein, with attack unless he withdrew from Kuwait. Like most other American politicans, Jackson immediately announced his support of the president's actions in the Mideast.

By mid-August, it was clear that Hussein was not going to retreat. Moreover, he announced that several thousand Americans and other foreign nationals were not free to return home. They were, in no uncertain terms, hostages.

Jackson decided that what he had done for Robert Goodman in 1984 he could do for the

Like hundreds of others at the 1988 Democratic National Convention, Los Angeles delegates Lillian Mobley (left) and Marva Smith find themselves in tears as they listen to Jackson (opposite page) deliver his spellbinding address. Former president Jimmy Carter described the Jackson effort as "the best speech ever given at a convention."

As singer Roberta Flack, an old friend and political supporter of Jackson's, looks on with amusement, Jackson clowns backstage with Flavor Flav of the rap group Public Enemy. Jackson featured a broad variety of guests, ranging from entertainers to attorneys, from civil rights leaders to former members of the Ku Klux Klan, on "Jesse Jackson," the syndicated television talk show that he began in the fall of 1990.

hostages held by Iraq. In late August, he proposed a trip to Baghdad, where he would appeal to Hussein for release of at least some of the hostages. After receiving a positive response from Iraq, Jackson departed New York City with his son Jonathan and 13 others.

Within a week, Jackson was conducting a two-hour interview with Hussein. At its conclusion, Hussein grabbed his visitor's hand and said, "You will take the women and children who are allowed to leave, along with four of the men who appear to be sick." Even after getting Hussein's approval, however, Jackson had to spend many hours negotiating with uncooperative Iraqi officials.

Watching Jackson in action, journalist Milton Viorst found him to be "at his best." When Jackson dealt with the Iraqis, Viorst wrote later, "as nearly as I could grasp it, his technique consisted of measured drafts of pleading, rational argument, cajolery, flattery, and moral importuning."

A few days after his conversation with Hussein, Jackson left Baghdad in an Iraqi Air 747 loaded with nearly 300 American, British, and French hostages. It was a considerable accomplishment. Back home in the United States at long last, one hostage—perhaps speaking for all—cried, "Thank God and Jesse Jackson!"

Two months after returning from Baghdad, Jackson entered a new profession: television journalism. "Jesse Jackson," a talk show syndicated by the Time-Warner communications corporation and produced by Quincy Jones, debuted in October 1990. Aired on Sunday evenings, the program featured roundtable discussions of political issues high on its host's agenda.

An early "Jesse Jackson" show, for example, centered on civil rights and included such diverse voices as those of Louisiana State Representative and former Ku Klux Klan leader David Duke, feminist lawyer Gloria Allred, conservative columnist Richard Viguerie, and Kweisi Mfume, a Baltimore congressman and vice-chairman of the Congressional Black Caucus. "So many of the disfranchised have given me their support over the years," said Jackson. "If they look for the weekend TV show to discuss civil rights 1990, this is the only place they'll see it discussed in depth."

Indeed, Jackson's is the strongest and most eloquent voice reminding America that equality is still a goal, not a reality. Whatever his future holds, he is sure to remain a presence, a force, in American life. Poverty and racism will not soon disappear, and the people from whom Jackson comes, and for whom he speaks, will continue to need a champion.

Back in the spring of 1988, Jackson shared a platform in San Francisco with Andrew Young. Ever since the March day in 1965 when he had watched the tall young stranger from Chicago invite himself to address the crowd in Selma, Young had wondered about Jackson. Over the years, his doubts had persisted.

As Jackson talked, Young listened intently. When Jackson spoke of going to a place the other candidates had not—to the side of those dying from AIDS—Andrew Young, a man who had heard thousands and thousands of speeches, found himself moved to tears. When Jackson finished, the two men embraced.

That evening at his hotel, still feeling the emotion from Jackson's words, Young wrote a private note to his old comrade and had it delivered by hand. It read: "You make me feel proud and humble when I hear you speak. Martin would be proud, too. You have my full endorsement as the moral voice of our time." ❦

CHRONOLOGY

1941   Born Jesse Louis Burns on October 8 in Greenville, South Carolina

1957   Takes surname of adoptive father, Charles Jackson

1962   Marries Jacqueline Davis

1963   Graduates from North Carolina Agricultural and Technical State University; enrolls in Chicago Theological Seminary

1965   Leaves seminary in senior year to work with the Reverend Martin Luther King, Jr., and his Southern Christian Leadership Conference (SCLC); takes charge of Operation Breadbasket, the SCLC's economic arm

1971   Leaves SCLC to form Operation PUSH (People United to Serve Humanity)

1984   Runs for nomination as Democratic presidential candidate; secures release from Syria of captured U.S. pilot; loses nomination to Walter Mondale

1988   Runs for Democratic nomination; makes strong showing but loses to Michael Dukakis

1990   Arranges release of 300 hostages from Iraq; starts television talk show, "Jesse Jackson"; elected nonvoting Senate representative from Washington, D.C.

FURTHER READING

————————

Abernathy, Ralph David. *And the Walls Came Tumbling Down.* New York: HarperCollins, 1990.

Colton, Elizabeth. *The Jackson Phenomenon.* New York: Doubleday, 1989.

Garrow, David. *Bearing the Cross: Martin Luther King, Jr., and the Southern Christian Leadership Conference.* New York: Morrow, 1966.

Germond, Jack, and Jules Witcover. *Wake Us When It's Over: Presidential Politics of 1984.* New York: Macmillan, 1985.

————. *Whose Broad Stripes and Bright Stars? The Trivial Pursuit of the Presidency 1988.* New York: Warner Books, 1989.

Goldman, Peter, and Tom Mathews, et al. *The Quest for the Presidency: The 1988 Campaign.* New York: Simon & Schuster, 1989.

Henry, William A., III. *Visions of America: How We Saw the 1984 Election.* Boston: Atlantic Monthly Press, 1985.

House, Ernest L. *Jesse Jackson and the Politics of Charisma: The Rise and Fall of the PUSH/Excel Program.* Boulder, CO: Westview Press, 1988.

Landess, Thomas H. *Jesse Jackson and the Politics of Race.* Ottawa, IL: Jameson Books, 1985.

McKissack, Patricia C. *Jesse Jackson: A Biography.* New York: Scholastic, 1991.

Reed, Adolph L., Jr. *The Jesse Jackson Phenomenon: The Crisis of Purpose in Afro-American Politics.* New Haven: Yale University Press, 1986.

Reynolds, Barbara. *Jesse Jackson: The Man, the Moment, the Myth.* Chicago: Nelson-Hall, 1975.

Sheehy, Gail. "Jesse Jackson: The Power or the Glory?" *Vanity Fair* 51 (January 1988).

Simon, Roger. *Road Show.* New York: Farrar, Straus & Giroux, 1990.

Stone, Eddie. *Jesse Jackson.* Los Angeles: Holloway House, 1988.

INDEX

PICTURE CREDITS

ROBERT JAKOUBEK holds degrees in history from Indiana University and Columbia University. He is coauthor of *These United States*, an American history textbook. For Chelsea House's BLACK AMERICANS OF ACHIEVEMENT series he has written *Joe Louis* and *Martin Luther King, Jr.*, the latter of which was selected by the National Council for the Social Studies and the Children's Book Council as one of the notable 1989 children's trade books in the field of social studies.

NATHAN IRVIN HUGGINS is W.E.B. Du Bois Professor of History and Director of the W.E.B. Du Bois Institute for Afro-American Research at Harvard University. He previously taught at Columbia University. Professor Huggins is the author of numerous books, including *Black Odyssey: The Afro-American Ordeal in Slavery*, *The Harlem Renaissance*, and *Slave and Citizen: The Life of Frederick Douglass*.